ヴィッキーの
ボジティブリスニング
100 Keys of Love

Vicki Bennett & Ian Mathieson

ポジティブな英語を聞いて、ポジティブな自分になる

英語とポジティブ思考を同時に手に入れる、ヴィッキーのセラピー・イングリッシュ

可能性に満ちた時代を生きる女性たち

　女性にとって、今ほど大変な時代はありません。仕事と私生活のバランスが求められるだけでなく、恋人、妻、母として、冷静かつ完璧であることを期待されています。女性たちの「賢く、美しくなければならない」というプレッシャーはとても大きなものです。

　しかし同時に、現代は女性にとってわくわくするような時代でもあります。多くの機会に恵まれ、さまざまな知識や情報にも簡単にアクセスすることができます。かつてないほど、皆が女性の声に耳を傾けています。組織のリーダー、政府の高官として世界的に活躍する女性も多く、女性の取締役も増えています。学校、仕事、パートナー、子供を持つかどうか——現代の女性は、そのような人生における選択の多くを、自分でできる時代に生きています。

　歴史的に見て、このように多くの選択肢が女性自身にゆだねられた時代はありません。私たちは自分を表現し、自分が望んだ人生を作り上げることができるのです。自己実現と成功、その希望あふれる時代に私たちは生きているのです。しかし逆から見れば、誰に頼ることもできない時代に女性は投げ出されてしまったともいえるでしょう。本書の執筆にあたり、私たちはこのような今までにない女性の環境に焦点をあて、アドバイスをしています。

つきない恋の悩み、人生への悩み

　私たちは、コンサルタントという仕事柄、何百人もの女性の悩みを聞いてきました。はたから見て、成功していると思える人でも、恋愛でひどく悩み、自分は幸福でないと感じている人はたくさんいます。逆に、それらの悩みを自分自身で上手に解決していける人もいます。

　礼儀正しい人、ユーモアがある人、不安定な人、情熱的な人、明るい人、やさしい人、怒りっぽい人、落ち込みがちの人、自信満々の人、シャイな人、幸福な人、悲しんでいる人、嫉妬深い人……そんなさまざまな側面を持つ女性たちですが、共通する性質が1つだけあります。それは、「好奇心」です。愛に、人生に、自分の可能性に、将来の選択に対する好奇心。それが女性の誰もが持っている性格ではないでしょうか。

　女性たちは皆、自分への好奇心にあふれています。だからこそ、皆が愛を探し、自分とは何かを探し続けています。本書の各章は、そのための道しるべとなっています。そして100のメッセージは、より豊かでポジティブな考え方ができるようにあなたを助けてくれるでしょう。この本で、自分とは何か、人生の中で自分が得たいものは何か、それ以外に何を見つけることができるのかを、探していただきたいと思います。

著者からのメッセージ

　私たちもこの本の執筆にあたり、たくさんの発見をしました。

　私たち夫婦は、22年前に出会いましたが、2人とも恋愛の秘訣、どうしたら2人でうまくやっていけるのかを知りませんでした。互いを愛する気持ちさえあれば、何もかも永遠にうまくいくと思い込んでいたのです。しかし今思うと、私たちの出会いは、「恋愛とは何か」を学ぶ始まりに過ぎませんでした。

2人の出会いは、恋愛という長い旅の始まりでした。相手をよく知り、相手が望んでいることは何か、必要なことは何かを話し合う。その過程で、多くの希望があり、そして絶望もありました。そして何よりも大きな気づきに満ちていました。私たちの関係は、Key of Loveを見つけるたびに、育ち、深まっていきました。

　また、たくさんの女性たちと話す中で、私たちは1人ではない、それぞれが愛と自分自身を探し続けているのだ、ということに気づかされました。この本はそうした自分探しの道しるべとなることでしょう。

　私たちの4人の娘は20代と30代で、この本を執筆するにあたり、今日の女性が直面する問題について、たくさんのアドバイスとフィードバックをくれました。強く、個性的で、ときに生意気な娘たちが、本書の執筆に貢献してくれたことをとてもうれしく思います。

　そして、私たちに心の内を語ってくれた多くの女性たちに感謝します。読者の皆さんが、本書によってあなただけの愛を見つけ、人生をより豊かでポジティブなものにできるよう、願ってやみません。

ヴィッキー・ベネット
イアン・マシスン

本書の効果的な使い方

ポジティブな英語を何度も聞こう

　試験のため、資格のため、日常会話のため……今までそれぞれの目的から、多くの教材をリスニング、ヒアリングのテキストに使用されてきたことと思います。その多くが、ニュースや新聞といった報道、映画やドラマの一場面、小説などの物語、ネイティブ同士の会話などではなかったでしょうか？　そしてその英語は、あなたの心に響くものでしたか？

　日本語の本をとっても分かるように、本のメッセージが心に届かなければ、どのような文章も生きた言葉として自分に吸収されることはありません。朝読んだ新聞記事の文章をもう思い出せないように（ましてやもう一度読みたいとは思わないように）、私たちが思っている以上にヒアリングやリスニングにおける「メッセージ性」は重要です。メッセージが強く、自分に届くものであればあるほど、あなたの耳はその言葉をとらえることができるのです。そして、繰り返し聞こうという気持ちも起こってくるはずです。

　本書はオーストラリアで人気のコンサルタントであり、若い人たちのカウンセラーも務めるヴィッキー・ベネットとイアン・マシスンの2人が、日本の読者、とりわけ女性に向けて書き下ろしたものです。恋の悩みを中心として、困難の多い現代を、いかに自分らしく生きていくかが主題となっています。日本人の読者向けに、難しい単語を使っていないというのは、私たち学習者にとって大きな助けとなります。そして、彼らの本の人気の大きな理由として、文章によるセラピー効用があります。本書の英文は私たちの心を癒やし、勇気づけ、前に進ませる気づきに満ちています。

　英語の実力を上げるために英語を聞かねばならないとしたら、無味乾燥な文章の羅列を頭に流し込むより、ポジティブで明日の元気にもとになる英語を自分にプレゼントしてはいかがでしょうか？　英語の実力とポジティブ思考を同時に手に入れること、それが本書の目標です。

本書の構成

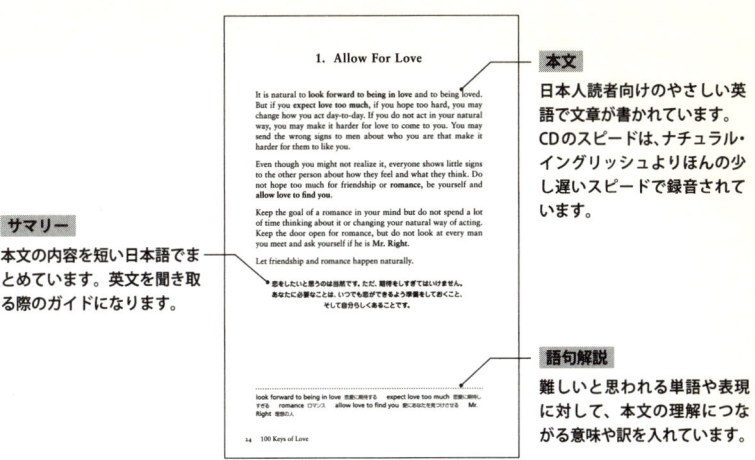

本文

日本人読者向けのやさしい英語で文章が書かれています。CDのスピードは、ナチュラル・イングリッシュよりほんの少し遅いスピードで録音されています。

サマリー

本文の内容を短い日本語でまとめています。英文を聞き取る際のガイドになります。

語句解説

難しいと思われる単語や表現に対して、本文の理解につながる意味や訳を入れています。

本文について

この本で、ぜひたくさんのポジティブな単語や表現に接してください。そして自分の中に、ポジティブな英語表現のストックを増やしておきましょう。

サマリーについて

各ページには文章のサマリーが日本語で書かれています。聞く前、もしくは聞きながら文章にさっと目を通しておくと、リスニングの手助けとなるでしょう。また、まずリスニングをしてから、文章の主題を理解できていたかを確認するツールとしてもお使いいただけます(本書には本文の全訳はありません)。

語句解説について

難しいと思われる単語や表現を本文理解の助けとなるように示しています。学習本のように「look forward to -ing 〜を楽しみに待つ」といった表記の仕方ではなく、「look forward to being in love 恋愛に期待する」というように、直接本文の翻訳にあたる解説を入れています。

INTRODUCTION

何度も繰り返し聞き、メッセージに触れる
この本は中学レベルの、やさしい英単語を使って執筆されています。初めからすべての文章を理解する必要はありません。何度かCDを聞いているうちに、メッセージは自然と理解されるようになるでしょう。またそれが英語であるからこそ、あなたの脳にとってもインパクトのあるメッセージとなるはずです。

　英語はポジティブな言語です。そして英語で書かれた本書のポジティブなメッセージは、あなたの心にしみ込み、あなたを元気にし、気持ちを前向きにしてくれるはずです。

学習方法
皆さんのレベルや目的によって、本書の使い方はさまざまです。もちろん下記の方法を組み合わせることも可能です。ぜひご自身の好きな方法を見つけ、本書をご活用ください。

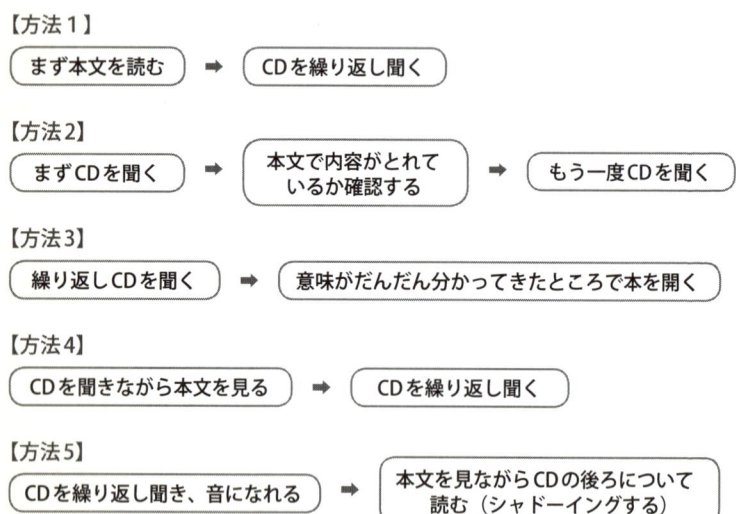

CDについて

本書の録音は、Vanessa Anthonyさんによるものです。彼女の声はとてもやさしく、心に響く特別なもの。柔らかい声で、聞く人の心を癒やしてくれます。

- ●アメリカ英語（女性ナレーター）
- ●収録時間　　Disc 1　約59分
- 　　　　　　　Disc 2　約57分
- ●スピード　　ナチュラル・イングリッシュより少し遅め
- ●収録内容　　本文の英語テキスト

✧ Contents ✦

SECTION 1
FINDING LOVE
恋を見つける

1. **Allow For Love** — 24
   恋に備える
2. **Falling In Love** — 25
   恋に落ちる
3. **Perfect Love?** — 26
   完璧な恋愛？
4. **What Men Want** — 27
   男性が望むこと
5. **What Women Want** — 28
   女性が望むこと
6. **Keep In Touch With What's Real** — 29
   真実から目をそむけない
7. **The Strength Of Being Alone** — 30
   1人でいる強さ
8. **Understand Yourself First** — 31
   まず自分を理解する
9. **Free Will** — 32
   自由な意志
10. **Fate** — 33
    運命

❦ Contents ❧

SECTION 2
FALLING IN LOVE
恋に落ちる

11.	**Romantic Love** ロマンティックな恋愛	36
12.	**Enjoy Your New Love** 新しい恋を楽しむ	37
13.	**Open Your Heart** 心を開く	38
14.	**Listen To Yourself** 心の声を聞く	39
15.	**Commit With Passion** 情熱を維持する努力	40
16.	**Take Your Time** 時間をかける	41
17.	**Check Reality** 現実を見つめる	42
18.	**Don't Rush Love** 恋は焦らず	43

❦ Contents ❧

SECTION 3
WHEN LOVE IS NEW
始まったばかり

19.	Understand Each Other 互いを理解する	46
20.	Grow The Relationship 関係を育てる	47
21.	Build Trust 信頼を築く	48
22.	Choose Your Feelings 気持ちを選ぶ	49
23.	Enjoy Yourself 自分自身を楽しむ	50
24.	Ask Questions 質問する	51
25.	Don't Jump Ahead Of Yourself 先のことを考えすぎない	52
26.	Be Yourself In Your Relationship 彼の前でもあなたらしく	53

Contents

SECTION 4
KEEPING THE FLAME OF LOVE ALIVE AND HEALTHY
愛を育む

27.	Forgiveness 許す	56
28.	Goals With Regard To Your Partner's Parents And Family 私と彼と彼の家族	57
29.	Goals For Happiness 幸せのゴール	58
30.	Show Compassion 思いやりの心を示す	59
31.	Keep Alive A Strong Vision For Your Love 恋の未来を思い描く	60
32.	Make Love The Goal 恋愛にも目標を	61
33.	80% Positive 80%ポジティブ	62
34.	Tell The Truth 本音を話す	63
35.	Ask For The Truth 本音を尋ねる	64

❀ Contents ❀

36.	**Let Go Of Control** コントロールしない	65
37.	**Learn From Each Other** 互いに学び合う	66
38.	**Look For Happiness** 幸せを探す	67
39.	**Do Nice Things For Your Partner** 彼の喜ぶことをする	68
40.	**Touch Your Partner Often** スキンシップ	69
41.	**Listen Carefully Before You Speak** 話す前によく聞く	70
42.	**Be Friends As Well As Lovers** 恋人であり同時に友人である	71
43.	**Listen To Your Inner Wisdom About Love** 内なる声に耳を傾ける	72
44.	**Look For Things You Really Like About Each Other** 長所を見つける	73
45.	**Have Loving Thoughts About Each Other** 思いやりを持つ	74
46.	**Keep A Clear Picture Of Your Love** 理想をはっきりと思い浮かべる	75
47.	**Accept Differing Ideas And Beliefs** 違いを受け入れる	76

ᴄᴙ Contents ʙᴐ

48.	**Balance The Way You Talk** 話し方に要注意	77
49.	**Love Can Be All That You Hope For** 愛は望みどおりに	78

SECTION 5
THROUGHOUT IT ALL
どんなときでも

50.	**Learn From Everything** すべてのことから学びを得る	80
51.	**Move Past Anger** 過去の怒りを忘れる	81
52.	**Teach Each Other** 互いに教え合う	82
53.	**Dealing With Difficult Times** 困難な時期に立ち向かう	83
54.	**Moving Forward** 前に進む	84
55.	**Don't Hold Back Your Love** 気持ちを抑え込まない	85
56.	**Trying To Please Everyone Doesn't Work** 皆を喜ばせようとしない	86

✧ Contents ✧

57.	**No-one Stays The Same** 人は変わる	87
58.	**Stay Connected To Your Feelings** 自分の心の声に常に耳を傾ける	88
59.	**When You Decide To Act On Your Feelings** 気持ちに正直に	89
60.	**When You Think Too Much** 考えすぎてしまうとき	90
61.	**Don't Try To Change The Other Person** 相手を変えようとしない	91
62.	**Don't Put Others Before Yourself** 人を自分より優先しない	92
63.	**Have Energy For Yourself** 自分のためのエネルギー	93
64.	**Distance Yourself From Friends You Cannot Trust** 信用できない友人と距離をとる	94
65.	**Be Careful How People Talk To You** 友人が言うことに注意する	95

❦ Contents ❧

SECTION 6
WHEN LOVE IS OVER
愛が終わったら

66.	**Freedom Of Choice** 選択の自由	98
67.	**Know When To Leave** 去り際を知る	99
68.	**Stop Blaming** 責めるのをやめる	100
69.	**When Things Are Finally Over** 本当に終わってしまったら	101
70.	**The Steps Of Grief** 悲しみの段階	102
71.	**Look To The Future With Hope** 希望を持って将来を見つめる	103
72.	**Try Something New** 新しいことにチャレンジする	104
73.	**Do Something Kind For Someone Else** 人にやさしく	105

Contents

SECTION 7
LOVING YOURSELF
自分を好きになる

74. How You See Yourself — 108
鏡に映る自分

75. Don't Compare Yourself With Others — 109
他人と比べない

76. Be Positive About Yourself — 110
自分にポジティブになる

77. Mistakes Are Great — 111
間違いはすばらしいこと

78. Don't Beat Yourself Up About Mistakes — 112
間違えた自分を責めない

79. Be Careful About Who You Spend Time With — 113
一緒に過ごす人に注意する

80. Have A Healthy Body — 114
健康な体

81. Don't Be Competitive With Friends — 115
友人と競わない

82. Move Your Body — 116
体を動かす

83. Relax — 117
リラックス

∽ Contents ∾

84.	**Have Fun** 楽しみを持つ	118
85.	**Sit Well And Stand Tall** きちんと座り、すっと立つ	119
86.	**Learn To Breathe Correctly** 正しく呼吸する	120
87.	**Time For Yourself** 自分のための時間	121
88.	**Do You Get Too Stressed?** ストレス過剰	122
89.	**Nurture A Healthy Self-image** 健全なセルフイメージを育む	123
90.	**Build Your Self-esteem** 自尊心を持つ	124
91.	**Take Control** コントロールする	125
92.	**Don't Shoot The Messenger!** メッセンジャーを撃たない	126
93.	**Learn To Like Yourself** 自分を好きになること	127
94.	**When You Are On Your Own You Can Learn And Grow** 1人で学び成長する	128
95.	**Connect With Yourself** 自分とつながる	129

∞ Contents ∞

96. Your Needs Are Important   130
   必要なことが大切なこと

97. Balance Your Needs   131
   ときには自分を優先する

98. Your Best Friend   132
   ベストフレンド

99. Speak Well To Yourself   133
   自分にやさしく語りかける

100. Success Starts With You   134
   成功はあなたから始まる

100 Keys of Love

Vicki Bennett & Ian Mathieson

SECTION

ෲ *1* ෯

FINDING LOVE

*'Take spring when it comes and rejoice.
Take happiness when it comes and rejoice.
Take love when it comes and rejoice.'*

Carl Ewald

1. Allow For Love

It is natural to **look forward to being in love** and to being loved. But if you **expect love too much**, if you hope too hard, you may change how you act day-to-day. If you do not act in your natural way, you may make it harder for love to come to you. You may send the wrong signs to men about who you are that make it harder for them to like you.

Even though you might not realize it, everyone shows little signs to the other person about how they feel and what they think. Do not hope too much for friendship or **romance**, be yourself and **allow love to find you**.

Keep the goal of a romance in your mind but do not spend a lot of time thinking about it or changing your natural way of acting. Keep the door open for romance, but do not look at every man you meet and ask yourself if he is **Mr. Right**.

Let friendship and romance happen naturally.

> 恋をしたいと思うのは当然です。ただ、期待をしすぎてはいけません。
> あなたに必要なことは、いつでも恋ができるよう準備をしておくこと、
> そして自分らしくあることです。

---

look forward to being in love 恋愛に期待する　　expect love too much 恋愛に期待しすぎる　　romance ロマンス　　allow love to find you 愛にあなたを見つけさせる
Mr. Right 理想の人

2. Falling In Love

Falling in love is a very special feeling; it is exciting, **pleasing,** and perhaps very new to you. Sometimes it also **makes you worry about the future**. It asks for new trust and **new sharing** and it makes you think about your sense of control over your life. Suddenly **your life seems to be rushing off** in new ways without you having control over it.

There is something special about the romance that comes with falling in love, with the opening of your heart to another person. Your dreams will change and your thoughts will also change; you will dream about what may happen with your new love and with the person you are falling in love with, and your thoughts will turn so often to that person. What is he doing right now? What is he thinking?

What you do each day will also change. You will plan with this new person to meet for coffee or to sit in the park. You will want to think ahead and make special plans, or to find a special moment such as buying a card to say how much you love that person.

Enjoy these **emotions** and thoughts; it is a very special time in your life. Let your whole being enjoy the beauty of falling in love.

恋をすることで、あなたの毎日が、将来の夢が、変化していくかもしれません。
恋をするというのは特別なことです。まずはその感情を思い切り楽しみましょう。

....

pleasing 楽しい   makes you worry about the future 将来の不安を感じさせる
new sharing 新しく共有すること   your life seems to be rushing off 毎日が忙しくなる
emotions 感情

3. Perfect Love?

Love is a very special feeling. Much is talked about romance as being perfect, but having that special feeling all the time is not possible. Someone else cannot make you feel special all of the time and you can't make someone else happy all of the time.

Women will be disappointed if they **search for the 'perfect' love,** where everything is great and the other person is thinking and **caring about** you all the time. It's easy to **lose your sense of reality** and come to hope too much for this kind of love, as your heart will be excited and your hopes will be high.

If you can have good feelings about yourself when you are falling in love, if you can care about and love yourself, if you can accept that love isn't perfect all the time, then you will allow love to happen in a more natural and caring way.

完璧な恋愛などありません。
そのことを受け入れたとき、もっと自然なやさしい形で恋愛が始まるのです。

---

women will be disappointed 女性はがっかりする　**search for the 'perfect' love** 「完璧な」恋愛を探す　**(is) caring about** 大切にしている　**lose your sense of reality** 現実を見失う

4. What Men Want

It is impossible to understand what goes on in someone else's mind. Women often try to guess what men want, without asking them.

Never try to guess what a man might want in a relationship. If you are in a relationship or starting a relationship, ask him. Ask gently, let him know that you care about him and wish to care for his needs.

Many men are not very confident about relationships and do not have a clear idea about what they want. Most men will welcome being asked and will **welcome the opportunity to talk** about their needs. Such discussion may also start him talking about your needs in a relationship.

There is no one answer to the question about what men want. Many things are written and said about what men want, especially in popular magazines and on TV. Most of these things are wrong. Every man is different and every man's needs are different.

Try not to listen to talk about what men want from other people or from TV or magazines. If you need to know what your man wants, ask him.

彼が望んでいることを知りたいなら、
想像するのではなく、質問することです。

....

many men are not very confident about relationships 多くの男性は2人の関係にしっかりとした自信を持っているわけではない　　welcome the opportunity to talk 会話の機会を喜ぶ

5. What Women Want

What other women want should **not matter to you**. You are not the same as other women, you are you. The question is 'What is it you want?' and being able to **express** this is much more important.

What you are told about other women and their wants is probably not what you feel your needs are. It is **far too easy** to **allow your thinking to be changed** from what you really want to what others tell you that you should want. Often people copy their thoughts or hopes from people on TV, the Internet or magazines, and those hopes or thoughts are not really their own.

Think about what you want for yourself. **What will suit you**; make you happy or pleased with your life? What are your plans, your hopes; what is your picture of the future? Keep your own thoughts close to you and talk with your friends or your partner about your dreams and hopes, not the ideas that come from other people and magazines.

Are you clear about what you want? Take some time to think about this very important question. You may find that your thoughts about what you want will change over time; these thoughts will change and grow as time passes. Be prepared for such change. The important thing is to remember your own hopes and dreams, not those of someone else.

あなたの欲しいものは、他の人とは違うはずです。

....

not matter to you あなたにとってはどうでもいい　　**express** 表現する　　**far too easy** あまりにも簡単　　**allow your thinking to be changed** あなたの考えを変えさせること　　**what will suit you** 何があなたにぴったりか

6. Keep In Touch With What's Real

At times in your life you can easily believe things that are not real or true for you. Other people's ideas will **influence you**. Ideas can come into your mind that seem to be OK at the time but later you might ask yourself, 'Why did I think like that?'

This happens often in life. It is easy for this to happen. But you can find ways to keep joined with what's real and true for you.

One way is to stop every now and again and ask yourself some simple questions. 'Am I clear about what I am thinking? Are there any little things that worry me at the moment? Are any of my family and friends asking me questions that **upset me**?'

Another way is to ask your partner, a friend or someone in your family to sit with you and talk about your life. Ask someone you can trust. From time to time, talk with them about whether your life is meeting your hopes and vision. Talk about whether you are happy or not.

Encourage honesty within yourself. Work out your own way to keep in touch with what's real in your life.

周りから影響を受けすぎてはいませんか。
何が大切なのか、じっくり考えましょう。

---

keep in touch with 理解し続ける　　influence you あなたに影響を与える　　upset me 私を動揺させる　　Encourage honesty within yourself. 正直である勇気を持ちましょう。

7. The Strength Of Being Alone

Learn how to enjoy being in your own company. You can learn so much about yourself when you spend time alone, listening to your own thoughts. Get to know yourself as you would a close friend. Spend some time alone to get to know yourself better.

If you look for a relationship to fill an empty space within you it won't always make you happy. The person may not be who or what you think they are or you may not be who or what they really want.

If that space in you is filled with love for yourself then when you do find someone to love, the relationship can start from **strength and equality** rather than **needing and wanting** someone to make you happy. If you already like yourself, the other person liking or loving you is an added happy event.

Even if you are happy in a relationship, you may welcome having time alone from time to time.

1人でいる時間はとても大切です。
自分と向かい合い、より自分自身を知るきっかけにもなります。

---

strength and equality 強さと対等   **needing and wanting** 必要と不足

8. Understand Yourself First

Take time to understand yourself first. Most women don't think their own needs and feelings are important. It takes time and effort to **get to know yourself well**.

Think about what you want and how you feel. Take care that you do not let your thoughts and actions about another person pull you **ahead of getting to know yourself first**. The more you know and like yourself, the more chance the relationship has of success.

Your partner will want to get to know who you are, so it is important to have taken the time to work that out and to be clear about who you are and what you want. When you share this with another person they will be meeting the real you, the true you.

> 多くの女性は自分のことを後まわしにしてしまいます。あなた自身が何を求め、何を思っているのか。自分のことをもっと知りましょう。

---

get to know yourself well 自分のことがよく分かるようになる **ahead of getting to know yourself first** 自分自身を知るより先に

9. Free Will

Free will is your ability to make a decision by yourself for yourself. When you use free will you choose to do something, or not do something, because of your own thoughts and experiences.

The difference between animals and humans is a human's ability to make decisions and use their free will to choose the best thing to do at any moment.

Do you use your own free will in your relationships? Do you listen to your experience, your wisdom, your understanding of things and trust yourself to make the right decisions for your life? When you listen, **your own inner thoughts and feelings** guide you to know the very best thing for you to do.

Using free will is like exercising your body. If you don't exercise your body you will lose some of your strength and it may not work as well as it could. Free will needs to be used every day for it to be a strength in your life. Use it every day.

強く生きるためには、あなたの意志が大切です。
人生において、何をして、何をしないかは、
あなた自身の決断で選び取るものだからです。

---

free will is your ability 自由な意志はあなたの能力である　　your own inner thoughts and feelings あなたが心の中で考えていること、感じていること

10. Fate

Fate is often a word used to explain something that has happened that seems to be out of your control. Fate is the idea of something happening that is bigger or better than your own free will.

Some people **leave their whole lives up to fate** and some leave their love lives up to fate… Others believe they control their lives through free will. Get to know which of these two you use and trust.

Tuck, a young woman in her 20's, talked about fate and her boyfriend. 'When I met him, I knew it was fate. I wasn't meant to be at the bus stop. It wasn't a bus stop I had ever been to before. I was there because I was late and a friend dropped me there to catch my bus and I started talking to this man because he was waiting for a bus there also. So I met my boyfriend because of fate, so the relationship must have been meant to happen.'

Fate can be things happening that are **out of the ordinary** or happy accidents or something that seems really unusual. These things that are called fate can lead to happy relationships sometimes, sometimes not.

Fate may draw you together in the first place, but your free will to act and react **in certain ways** will be what keeps you together.

運命を生かせるかどうかは、あなた次第です。

---

leave their whole lives up to fate 人生のすべてを運命にまかせる　　out of the ordinary 日常とは違って　　in certain ways 何らかの形で

SECTION

☙ 2 ❧

FALLING IN LOVE

*'We waste time looking for the perfect lover,
instead of creating the perfect love.'*

Tom Robbins

11. Romantic Love

The idea of romantic love is a strongly held belief in most women. Many women dream of a man coming into their life and falling in love with them and everything being OK forever.

The dream of falling deeply in love easily and **living happily ever after** is common among women. This is not how it happens most of the time. Love can be difficult and painful at times and it can be hard to go on loving someone. After a time the first stage of romance can leave the relationship and change into a different kind of love and you may miss that new falling-in-love feeling. Some people just keep changing partners because they only want to feel that first falling-in-love feeling.

Most people **in long-term relationships** still enjoy romantic feelings from time to time—unlike new love, where **the first falling-in-love feeling** seems to be there all the time.

Falling in love is just the first step in a relationship, not the whole of the relationship. If you have **the courage to accept** that love changes over time, and journey through the changes in that love, a deeper love and pleasure will come from the relationship.

恋に落ちたときだけが、恋愛のすべてではありません。
出会った頃のときめきはなくても、その後には形を変えた大きな愛や喜びが
あなたを待っているのです。

---

living happily ever after 一生幸せに暮らす　　in long-term relationships 長いつき合いの中で　　the first falling-in-love feeling 恋に落ちたときの最初の気持ち　　the courage to accept 受け入れる勇気

12. Enjoy Your New Love

There is no special way to love someone, but some people find it difficult to **open their hearts to love.**

'I was always fearful of opening myself up to love. I had seen my mother get hurt over and over again as I was growing up and I didn't have much trust in relationships. So when I met someone I liked I would not open my heart and they would see this as me not being interested in them and walk away from me and any kind of relationship with me. It was hard for me just to be open and take a chance.'

Ono

Being in the moment with that special person, smiling and being present for them is a great start. Opening your heart to the other person is **a positive way to find the love** in your heart.

心を開くことが難しいこともあります。
でもそうすることで、新しい恋はスタートするのです。

---

open their hearts to love 恋愛に心を開く　　a positive way to find the love 愛を見つけるポジティブな方法

13. Open Your Heart

Many women are afraid to open their heart and trust another person **just in case they are hurt**. The risk may seem to be high; if you love someone, **you take the risk of being hurt or rejected**.

Some people ask us what it is like to really open your heart to someone. Adrienne told us this story. 'To open my heart for me is like when my four-year-old niece comes running up the stairs to say, "Hi." I see her and my heart is full of love and happiness. That to me is opening my heart. To just feel open and loving and **not expect anything in return**.'

Opening your heart to love and another person **takes courage**. There is always a risk that love will not succeed and you will be hurt, but falling in love without opening your heart is like having sushi without wasabi. One doesn't really work without the other.

人を愛すれば、傷つくこともあります。
これ以上傷つかないために、心を閉ざしてはいませんか。

---

just in case they are hurt 万が一傷ついたときのために　　you take the risk of being hurt or rejected 傷つけられたり拒絶されたりするリスクを負う　　not expect anything in return 見返りに何も求めない　　takes courage 勇気がいる

14. Listen To Yourself

It can be difficult when you are falling in love to keep your mind clear and open to hear **your own inner wisdom**.

Love can make it difficult to make up your mind about what to do and what not to do. Sometimes you will want to ask someone else about what you should do. If you do this, remember that mostly they will tell you what they would do in the same situation. Hardly ever does the other person think about what is really best for you.

Let's say you tell a friend that you want to live with your boyfriend and that you are leaving home to do this. For them, it may seem to be the worst choice in the world and very stressful and they will advise you not to do it. They will talk about their fears and their worries.

They might say, 'You are doing the wrong thing, moving in with him,' or plant **the seed of doubt** by asking, 'Are you sure you know what you're doing?' What they really mean to say is, 'The thought of doing that makes me feel uneasy because I couldn't do it, so don't talk with me about doing it.' They mostly give their view.

Trust and listen to the advice from others, but always make your own decisions, following your own inner wisdom. If you listen to your feelings, your inner wisdom will guide you to solve your own issues and problems.

人のアドバイスに惑わされず、自分自身で決めることが大切です。

---

your own inner wisdom あなたの内にある賢明さ　　the seed of doubt 疑問の種

15. Commit With Passion

Passion can easily be lost when you get used to each other in a relationship. Talking, listening and spending time together are all ways to **reconnect with the passion** you felt at the start of a relationship.

Connect with your passion by having more fun, being warm and close, sharing your thoughts of love, thinking kindly and being caring for your partner. Plan things to create this passion: plan surprises, special dates or **outings together**, touch more, laugh more, and do things for the other person that they are not expecting. This is how you create more passion in your life.

情熱を維持するには、努力が必要です。
サプライズや特別なデートのプランを立てましょう。
彼が予想もしなかったことを計画してみましょう。

---

commit with passion 情熱を維持する　　reconnect with the passion 再び情熱を持つ
outings together 一緒に出かける

16. Take Your Time

It takes time to get to know another person well; possibly a whole lifetime. Make the time to get to know someone well first before you make the choice to be with them forever. Don't **rush into a serious relationship** too fast. Sometimes the person you fall in love with may not be the type you would have expected to love. It can be very surprising who you fall in love with.

When you are first in love it is very easy not to notice things about the other person that you may not like. Love has a way of making you **blind to the other person's faults.**

The other person may be getting used to his own feelings; his feelings may be new to him also. He may need to match these feeling with yours and need time to do this. When you take your time to get to know someone well it helps friendship to grow between you and gives your relationship a good chance to be a success.

相手を知るには、時間がかかります。焦って先に進もうとしないことです。

---

rush into a serious relationship 焦って深い関係になる   blind to the other person's faults 相手の欠点が全く見えない

17. Check Reality

How do you check that your relationship is what you think it is? When love is new and strong and passionate it is hard to stop and check your feelings deeply. If your thoughts become unclear and you don't know if your relationship is right for you, this is the time to give yourself a reality check.

'I was so in love I just went along with everything my boyfriend wanted. I had a small feeling that something wasn't right in our relationship, but I just didn't want to look too closely at it for fear it may **unravel the whole of the relationship**. It turned out he had a wife and child in another town and I was **just a bit of fun to him**.'

Tay

Take the time to talk and listen. Ask the hard questions to really get to know the other person.

少しでも疑問を感じたら、現実を見つめる努力をしましょう。

---

unravel the whole of the relationship 関係が完全にだめになる　　just a bit of fun to him 彼にとってただの遊びである

18. Don't Rush Love

When you rush into a relationship it can blind you to the other person as they really are and you may lose contact with your own feelings and values. Everyone needs time to think about their own needs and about what the other person is really like and to get to know them.

Find out about the other person—the things they think are important to them, the things they love and hate, like and dislike. **Put your feelings on hold** until you have worked out more about them.

It can be hard to do this because passion and love can be very strong and you may not want to go slowly. You may not see everything there is about the other person. It is very important to balance passion with getting to know the other person.

焦らずに。情熱に振り回されてはいけません。

---

put your feelings on hold 気持ちを抑える

SECTION

⊛ *3* ⊛

WHEN LOVE IS NEW

'We can only learn to love by loving.'

Iris Murdoch

19. Understand Each Other

Everyone is different. There are no two people who have the same likes or the same dislikes. Each person has had their own life which is different from everyone else's. Your partner or boyfriend will probably have had a very different life than you. Sometimes that is just the thing that brings you together **in the first place**.

The only way you can learn to understand about another person is to ask them about themselves and to really listen to them when they tell you. **Try to picture what their life has been like** and understand where they have come from. When you listen to someone **with all your attention** you will understand them better and they will respect you more. They in turn may listen to you more when you choose to speak.

1人として同じ人はいません。
相手を知るためには、質問し、話を聞くことです。

---

in the first place まず初めに　　**try to picture what their life has been like** 彼らの生活がどのようなものであったか思い描く　　**with all your attention** 最大の注意を払って

20. Grow The Relationship

When you are in love and love is new, there can be a feeling that life is moving quickly and everything is rushing forward. There can be much excitement in your heart and your mind, and this is great. But it is very easy to let **this excitement carry you along** without thinking about where the relationship is going and how it is to be carried forward.

When this happens to you, think about what you and your partner can do to grow the relationship together. Think about asking your new partner to discuss and plan things together and find shared goals. Let him know the things that are important to you. Help him to understand your needs, and learn how to ask him to understand your needs. Talk together about growing the friendship between you.

These things will help you and your partner to grow your new relationship.

2人の関係を育てるために、話し合いましょう。
あなたが大切に思っていることを、分かってもらうのです。

---

this excitement carry you along 興奮があなたを押し流す

21. Build Trust

Trust between two people can grow; it can grow as you get to know each other better and as you learn how to talk together about difficult things that happen. Talking through events that have happened which are harder for you to deal with builds trust between people.

It is sometimes natural to try to hide some things from your partner. You might want to **keep things from your partner** that you think might make you look bad or show you to be weak or unable to make choices or plans.

You will lessen your partner's trust if you hide these things from him. Your partner will know either in his mind or in his heart that you are keeping some important things from him and this will take away his trust.

Build trust by being open with your partner about the things that are hard for you to share, as well as the things that are easy to share. Make a habit also of listening to him about the things that are hard for him to deal with.

相手の信用を得るためには、隠し事をしないことです。
隠しておきたいことこそ、伝えるのです。

---

keep things from your partner パートナーに秘密にしておく

22. Choose Your Feelings

We have heard women say, 'He made me feel bad' or, 'She made me feel sad.' No one can make you feel anything without your OK. You choose to feel good or bad about what has been said. The other person can't make you feel it, you do. In truth, people feel good or bad because of **what they say to themselves about what another person has said**.

If your partner says, 'I don't like what you are wearing' you can think, 'Well that's **his point of view** but I like it and I am happy with it and I am going to wear it'. Or you can say 'Why does he always hurt me with what he says, he doesn't love me, I look bad, I am not pretty.'

Wow! Two very different ways of thinking about what your partner said. The first one just says he can have that point of view, but you don't share it. The second makes the comment grow into a hurtful unkind view that may not even be true.

It is always what you say to yourself about what the other person has said that hurts the most, not what they really said to you.

本当にあなたを傷つけるのは、人の言葉ではありません。
その言葉を受けたあなた自身が、自分に投げつける言葉なのです。

---

what they say to themselves about what another person has said　人から言われたことを、自分自身に投げつけること　　his point of view　彼の考え方

23. Enjoy Yourself

Remember to enjoy yourself, to have fun, to be light and cheerful, at least most of the time.

There are times when you might not feel happy or times when you have things to worry about. You might have to work hard at times and focus strongly, but it is still possible to be happy and light.

There are many times when you could choose to be lighter and more cheerful. **This will help your spirit**; it will make you stronger and **more able to get along with others** when times are hard for you. Being light and happy makes you more pleasant with your family and friends. Sharing your fun and happiness with your partner can add to the enjoyment of both of you.

You can choose to enjoy yourself more, and to have more fun.

どんな時にも、できるだけ明るくいるように心がけましょう。
そうすることであなたは強くなり、
人との関係もうまくいくようになります。

---

this will help your spirit あなたの心の助けになる　　**more able to get along with others** 人とよりうまくやっていく

24. Ask Questions

Learn to ask questions about your partner. Show a real interest in what he thinks and feels. Don't be afraid to ask.

Some people don't find it easy to ask their boyfriend or partner about themselves. If you are one of these people, make the effort to do this. Ask questions such as, 'What are you feeling now?' or 'What is happening right now for you?' or 'Can I help you with anything?' Then listen to his answer. Really listen. Don't start asking another question or make a comment. Wait and **listen to him with all your heart**.

Learn to proceed quietly and be a loving, listening person. Grow your understanding, grow your friendship, and this will grow your love.

彼の考えていること、思っていることを尋ねることを怖がらないで。
そして質問をしたなら、彼の答えにじっと耳を傾けるのです。

---

listen to him with all your heart 心を込めて彼の話を聞く

25. Don't Jump Ahead Of Yourself

Everyone can do so much at a time; we are all able to think about many things at once. **Jumping ahead of what is happening at the moment** happens because you can think about many things at the same time, including thinking about the future. Thinking too much about the future will not support what you are doing right now.

'I am always thinking about tomorrow and when the day is over I feel unhappy because I haven't done much. I think it's because I think too much about tomorrow and not enough about what I am doing right now.'

Lon

Be aware of the present moment; give it your best, rather than going too far forward. Be aware and enjoy the present moment.

将来のことを考えすぎるのはやめましょう。
大切なのは今この瞬間です。

---

jumping ahead of what is happening at the moment　現在起きていることより先んじること　　be aware of the present moment　今この瞬間に目を向ける

26. Be Yourself In Your Relationship

Sometimes people try to act like something or someone they are not. Don't try to pretend that you are like another person. That is hard to keep up and **you do yourself harm by trying.**

Keep explaining your values, your thoughts to your partner. Your values and thoughts are very important as they become who you are.

You don't have to agree with the other person's values and thoughts to have a happy relationship. But you need to express your values and beliefs to give the other person the chance to understand who and what you are, even if they don't agree with you. You also need to think about how you can accept their values even if you don't agree with them.

別人であるかのようにふるまってはいけません。
相手に本当のあなたを分かってもらい、
あなたらしくいることこそが大切なのです。

---

you do yourself harm by trying そうしようとすることで自分を傷つける

SECTION 4

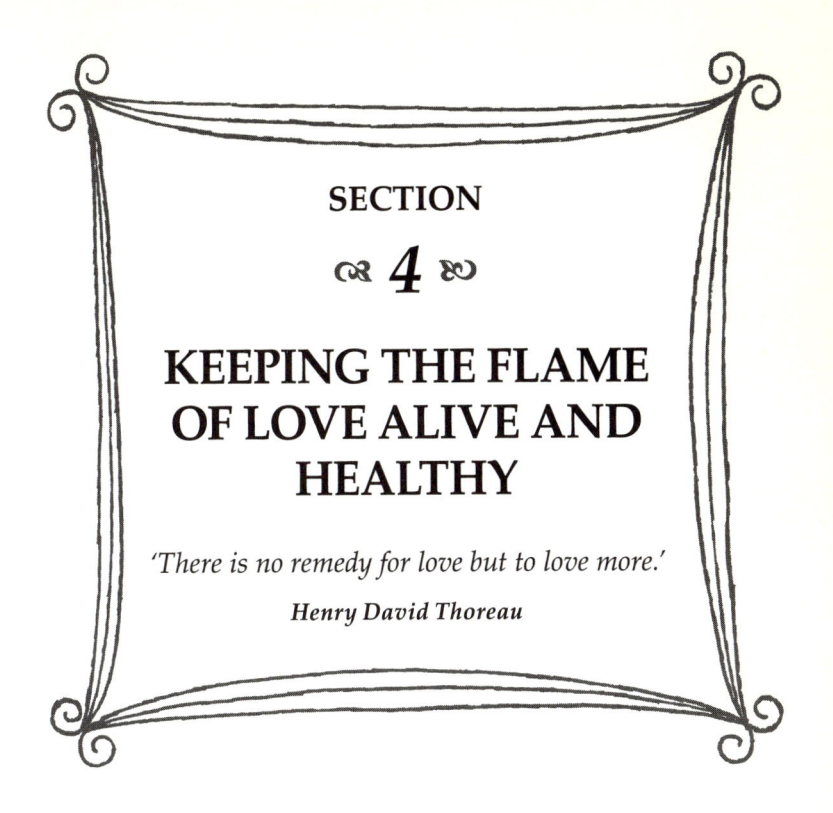

KEEPING THE FLAME OF LOVE ALIVE AND HEALTHY

'There is no remedy for love but to love more.'
Henry David Thoreau

27. Forgiveness

Everyone finds it hard to forgive someone who has done something that hurts you or something thoughtless. It is easy to **go on thinking** much too often about what it was they did to hurt you.

Doing so does not help you to **get on with your life**. It does not help you to live your life in a happy way. The other person might have hurt you once; but when you think about it over and over again, you hurt yourself again and again. Every time you think about it you **relive the hurt**. By reliving the pain in your mind over and over again, do you not hurt yourself more often than the other person **hurt you in the first place**?

Learn to forgive other people when you think they have hurt you or done something wrong to you. Also, learn to forgive yourself for things you have done wrong or could have done better.

The past is gone and finished. If you have done something wrong, learn from what you have done and try never to do it again. Forgive yourself and think about how you can be better in the future.

あなたを傷つけた人を許すのは難しいことです。
でも、その出来事を考え続けることが、
さらにあなたを傷つけていることに気づきましょう。

---

go on thinking 考え続ける　　get on with your life 人生を生きていく　　relive the hurt 再び傷つく　　hurt you in the first place 最初にあなたを傷つけた

28. Goals With Regard To Your Partner's Parents And Family

Having a relationship with one special person does not mean that the relationship is with that one person alone. They may have parents, brothers and sisters and other family. It is unusual to have a relationship without contact with your partner's family.

Keep in your mind that your partner's family has had a long relationship with him. They will know each other well and will have ways of talking with each other and doing things with each other. Remember also that they have their own ways to show their love for each other.

Do not feel strange or alone when you are with his family. Sometimes you may even think that they don't want you in their lives or the life of their son. Remember that they love him and want what they feel will be the best for him.

Try to understand them. Listen to them carefully and ask them questions so you may **come to know them better**. Do not feel that you need to own your partner and keep him apart from his family; show that you are happy to share him with his family.

彼を独り占めしようとしないこと。彼の家族のことを知る努力をしましょう。

---

keep in your mind 心に留めておく　　come to know them better 彼らをよく知るようになる

29. Goals For Happiness

Most people want to be happy in their lives. They want to be happy in their relationship, their work, their friendships and in the way they learn.

It can be too easy to think that having lots of money or lots of things will bring happiness. Most people who have lots of money or many things say that these do not bring happiness. They say that to have many things or lots of money leads them to worry about keeping their money or their things, more than enjoying them.

Think carefully about **what you would like to achieve in your life**—what you think would help you to be happy. Having some money and some things is important for you and it is valuable to have goals about these things.

Think about other parts of your life. Is good health important to you? Is a loving relationship important to you? Is it important to you to have some time to yourself every day? Do you have something you love to do? Do you read, paint, swim, dance, walk or enjoy doing something else?

Making goals for these things will help you to enjoy a balanced, happy life.

**お金や物があっても、幸せになれるとは限りません。
人生で本当に成し遂げたいことは何かを真剣に考えてみましょう。**

....

what you would like to achieve in your life 人生であなたが成し遂げたいこと

30. Show Compassion

Compassion is showing care and kindness to another person rather than being hard or distant and judging others in a hard way. It shows that you have a kind heart. Compassion for another person is finding the strength to care about them even when they have done something wrong, bad, or hurtful without thinking of you or of others.

Compassion guides you to listen to the other person and discuss their problems. Listening and really hearing can help you to understand them and to think kindly of them. Don't try to help them to find an answer to their problem; only they can do that. Listening with your heart open is **the valuable thing** to do for them and for you.

Compassion is also about being kind to yourself as well as being kind to the other person.

> 思いやりの心というのは、相手のことを考えられる強さのことです。
> そしてそれは、自分自身のことも大切にするということです。

---

show compassion 思いやりを示す   the valuable thing 価値のあること

4 KEEPING THE FLAME OF LOVE ALIVE AND HEALTHY

31. Keep Alive A Strong Vision For Your Love

Very often love starts out being exciting, fresh, new, fun and it can sometimes go on like this. It can be far too easy to **take the other person's love for granted**. If this happens, there is a risk that the love loses its energy and the relationship loses its hope for the future.

There are lots of ways to keep your love strong and healthy for the future and one of these is to keep alive a strong vision for your love. **A vision or picture of the future** as you would like it to be, of you and your partner.

Showing your love and friendship and enjoying each other is an example of a good vision for the future.

Share your vision with your partner. Talk with him about how he feels about your vision. Ask him if he shares this vision. Keep your vision fresh and alive.

情熱を保ち続ける方法の1つは、将来の夢を彼と語り合うことです。

---

take the other person's love for granted 相手の愛情を当然と思う　　a vision or picture of the future 将来への展望やイメージ

32. Make Love The Goal

Goals are important in any relationship. The best way to build your love together is to have positive goals, things you want or will do, rather than negative goals, things you don't want or want to stop doing.

Take time to **connect with your partner** and the love between you and make some goals together, such as how you are going to talk with each other, how much time you want to spend together, how you are going to grow the friendship between you, how you are going to show your love for each other.

Focus on what you want rather than what you don't want. Have some very clear goals about the love you want because this **helps your mind to stay clear and focused**. Your mind is always looking forward to a goal that is positive rather than a negative goal. Be careful to show your love as your number one goal.

> あなたがこうありたいと思う愛の形について、
> よりはっきりとした目標を持ちましょう。

---

connect with your partner パートナーと心を通わせる　　helps your mind to stay clear and focused 心をクリアにして集中させる助けとなる

33. 80% Positive

It is sometimes very easy to talk too much about the things that have gone wrong for you or have not been pleasant for you. If you speak mostly about all the negative things in your life or relationship, that is **how you will be seen by others**. It also is **how you will come to believe yourself to be**.

The things that have gone wrong for you are probably only a small part of what you have done. Most of the things you do are OK and you might feel happy about them. The things that have gone wrong in any day are probably less than 20% of what you have done in that day.

Make sure that you talk positively about the things that are OK for you or are good in the world. Make sure that what you talk about is at least 80% positive and less than 20% negative. You will feel happier and the world will seem a better place.

ネガティブなことばかり話してはいませんか。
会話の80%はポジティブな内容にしていきましょう。

---

how you will be seen by others　あなたが他の人にどのように見られるか　　how you will come to believe yourself to be　あなたが自分がどのような人であると思うようになるか

34. Tell The Truth

In a relationship it is important to **be honest with each other**, to tell the truth. If you don't tell the truth, your partner might see this as something wrong with the relationship. He might think you have something that is worrying you. He might think you don't trust him with your feelings, or that you are **keeping something from him.**

Let's say he asks you, 'Am I working too many long hours? Do you need me to spend more time with you?' You might think of saying, 'No, it's fine. Everything is OK'. He knows that he is never at home; he knows the hours he works are long. So if you don't tell him the truth, next time he asks you about something, he may question **whether you are trying to be nice to him** and whether he can trust your answer.

If you do not tell the truth, you might think that you are being kind to your partner, but you really are not being fair to him or to yourself. Tell the truth with kindness, but tell the truth.

本音を話すことはとても大切です。相手に遠慮してばかりではいけません。あなたが本当に思っていることを伝えるのです。

---

be honest with each other　お互いに正直である　　keeping something from him　彼に何か隠し事をする　　whether you are trying to be nice to him　彼にやさしくしようとしているのかどうか

35. Ask For The Truth

Sometimes your partner will say things to you to be nice or pleasant to you, rather than being 100% truthful.

You might be in a dress shop and you really like a dress. Let's say your partner is good at picking dresses that **look good on you**, and you ask him whether one suits you. He knows that this dress is not for you, perhaps the line just isn't right for your body or the color is wrong. If he's truthful he will say that it doesn't look exactly right for you. If he tries to please you, he might say that it looks good on you rather than tell you the truth.

Which would you rather hear?

Make it clear to your partner that you want him to be truthful with you every time, even if he thinks that **what he says may not be what you would like to hear**. Promise not to react badly if he tells you something you don't like.

彼にも本音で話してもらいましょう。
たとえあなたの望む答えではなくても、怒ったりしてはいけません。

---

look good on you　あなたに似合う　　what he says may not be what you would like to hear　彼の言うことはあなたの聞きたいことではないかもしれない

36. Let Go Of Control

Most people do not like being told what to do. When you tell someone what to do you may be trying to control them rather than wanting the best for them.

Controlling another person's actions and thoughts by trying to get them to act or think differently will not be successful **in the long term**. When one person tries to control the other, this makes a problem in the relationship. One person will be unhappy that **the other person will not do what they ask** and the other person will be unhappy that they are not trusted to make good choices.

Ask for the things you need in a relationship without trying to control what the other person says or does. This way, if the person does what you ask, they do it because they are free to do it, not because you are trying to control their actions and thoughts.

It is not possible to control another person; if you try, you will make them and yourself very unhappy.

> 人は命令されるのが嫌いです。相手をコントロールしようとしても、
> それは決して成功しないどころか、2人の関係を危うくします。

---

in the long term 長期的には   the other person will not do what they ask 相手が自分の言ったことをしない

37. Learn From Each Other

Throughout your life you will learn and go on learning. **Everything you do gives you a chance to learn** more about yourself. Being in a relationship is a great way to learn about yourself because when you are close to another person you notice things about them and you that are worth thinking about.

You will always learn from each other in relationships. You will notice things that happen and think about your feelings about these things. You may think about what you could do better next time and if you are brave enough, **you can change the way you do things for the better.**

This is how you learn from another person; by noticing your feelings and then changing the way you do things.

人とつき合うということは、自分を知るよいチャンスです。
相手から学び、よりよい方法を学ぶこともできるのです。

....

everything you do gives you a chance to learn　あなたがすることすべてが学ぶチャンスとなる　　you can change the way you do things for the better　あなたはよりよい方法に変えることができる

38. Look For Happiness

Everyone has a sense of happiness in them, of being able to look on the bright side of things. In your life, things that happen can sometimes be hard for you. You will have some good times and some difficult times, some good days and bad days.

When things are difficult for **some of the time** you will need to think about fixing whatever has caused the problem. You may think about what you can do differently or better next time.

At the same time you can choose not to over-worry about the problem; doing so can be a waste of your energy. Be lighter in your spirit during difficult times, both in your actions and your relationships. Choose not to think about the problems all the time, think about the happy things in your life and **be grateful for these happy things**.

You can choose to look for the happiness even when things are difficult.

> 常に何かに悩んでいると、生きるエネルギーが損なわれてしまいます。
> 人生のよい面を思い、そのことに感謝しましょう。

---

some of the time ときには **be grateful for these happy things** それらの幸福なことがらに感謝する

39. Do Nice Things For Your Partner

Remember to do nice things for your partner. Something thoughtful or pleasant will be thought of very kindly by your partner and will help the relationship to be healthy and grow.

When you do something pleasant you are showing that you love your partner and that you care so much for them that you wish to please them in small or big ways. Mostly, a small gift or act will be enough; **it does not need to cost a lot of money**. It is the thought that is important, the thought that shows your love.

Give your partner a small written note, or a card with a message of love, a book or a letter or some small thing that he likes. This will tell him how much you care for him. These are all small things that do not cost a lot of money but which show how much you love him.

Do nice things for your partner often.

> もっと彼を喜ばせましょう。お金をかける必要はありません。
> あなたが彼を喜ばせようとすることが、彼の心を動かすのです。

---

it does not need to cost a lot of money　たくさんお金をかける必要はない

40. Touch Your Partner Often

One of the things that babies and children value very much is the sense of touch. Being touched is important to them and to **their sense of well-being** and safety. As you grow up, this wonderful part of your life—touching, and being touched—may not happen as much. Somehow we get the idea it's not OK for grown-up people to touch so much.

Touch your partner often. A gentle touch on the arm or a soft touch to the face is friendly; it talks to both of you about your love and helps your well-being. Hold hands. Sit close when watching TV or when you are both sitting reading together. You may not be aware of how much a gentle touch can help you build your love for each other. **Your heart will recognize this touch** and it will add to building a loving relationship.

触れ合うことはとても大切です。
スキンシップは2人の愛を大きく育てます。

---

their sense of well-being 幸福で満ち足りた気持ち   your heart will recognize this touch あなたの心はこの触れ合いを感じる

4 KEEPING THE FLAME OF LOVE ALIVE AND HEALTHY

41. Listen Carefully Before You Speak

Your mind can bring up thoughts and pictures much faster than you can speak words. This is one reason that you might find it hard to listen fully when another person is talking. Your mind can easily move to other thoughts while the other person is speaking. Your mind can start to think about what you will have for lunch or what you will do when you get back to work.

It is very easy for you to **start to think ahead** while another person is speaking. It is easy to think of what you might say next after the other person has finished talking and it is **your turn to speak**.

Thinking too far ahead shows a lack of respect for the other person. Listen carefully and seek to understand the other person and it will show care that honors them. **The other person can sense** if you are not listening carefully. When you listen with care it helps to make a close and positive relationship.

Take special care to listen to your partner.

相手の話をちゃんと聞くことは、難しいものです。
だからこそ相手の話を注意深く聞く態度が、
相手への気持ちを示すことになるのです。

---

start to think ahead 次の事を考え始める　　your turn to speak あなたの話す番
the other person can sense 相手は気づくだろう

42. Be Friends As Well As Lovers

Love is the base for a successful relationship and friendship is the food that helps the relationship to grow and be healthy. This is a good balance; friendship and love together strengthen a relationship and help it to stay healthy and strong.

Love comes from a deep sense of togetherness and joining of the spirit or soul. Love is mostly about your feelings, **whereas friendship is very much about how you both get along together.** Long term success in a relationship **needs friendship as well as love.** Learning about the other person builds the friendship. You can grow the friendship by listening, being thoughtful, being helpful, being kind and caring.

Remember to keep friendship as a real part of your relationship, as well as love.

２人がよりよい関係を保つためには、愛情と同じく友情が必要です。
この２つのバランスがよければ、２人の関係はより強固なものになるのです。

....

whereas friendship is very much about how you both get along together 友情が互いに努力し合うものであるのに対し　　**needs friendship as well as love**　愛情と同じく友情が必要

43. Listen To Your Inner Wisdom About Love

When things aren't working in your relationship and it doesn't feel right, listen to your inner wisdom. Here are some ideas:

- Breathe deeply and listen to what's happening inside of you.

- Ask yourself, 'What is the best thing for me to do about this right now?' Let go and wait for an idea or thought to come. It might take minutes or days, but an answer will come.

- **Be alert** and look for answers around you; you may just feel a small understanding of what to do next.

- You may be talking with someone and they will say something that answers your question.

- Act upon this small understanding, do what you believe needs to be done.

Your inner wisdom often knows things that your thinking does not see or know.

Trust yourself because **no matter what advice you get from other people,** it is you that has to deal with your life and your relationships.

うまくいかないとき、何かがおかしいと感じるときには、
あなたの内なる賢明さに、静かに耳を傾けましょう。

---

listen to your inner wisdom　あなたの内にある賢明さに耳を傾ける　　be alert　注意する
no matter what advice you get from other people　他人からどんなアドバイスを得ようと

44. Look For Things You Really Like About Each Other

It is easy to be hurt by small things that your partner does. Thinking too much about these things can make you very unhappy. If you are not careful, bad feelings about small things can **come to be what you think about most of the time.**

Don't spend too much time thinking about all the small things that are bad about your partner. Balance this by thinking about what you really like and love about him. There will be much more that you like than you dislike.

Right now, think about three things that he does that are kind or are nice for you.

Learn to balance the small bad things with the good things he does. Learn to accept the small things because that is what they are... small things.

> 彼の些細な欠点を気にかけてばかりいませんか。
> 今すぐ、彼のいいところを3つあげてみましょう。
> そして欠点とのバランスを考えてみるのです。

---

come to be what you think about most of the time あなたの頭に常にあるようになる

45. Have Loving Thoughts About Each Other

Do you remember the dreams and passion you had at the start of your relationship? Do you believe that you should have this love always? Sometimes it is not as easy to feel this kind of love **on a day-to-day basis**. Everyday living sometimes puts to one side your dream of a great love.

Remind yourself daily to be loving and gentle with your partner so you can link yourself and him with your dream of love. Having loving thoughts about the other person helps you to be more loving and kind and is a healthy way to live your life.

When you think mostly of the good and positive things about your love you make it easier to accept and not worry about the small things you do not like.

恋愛が始まった頃の情熱を維持するのは難しいものです。
毎日の生活の中で、愛情あふれる思いやりの心を相手に示しましょう。
それがあなたを愛ある生活へと導きます。

---

loving thoughts 愛情あふれる思いやりの心　　**on a day-to-day basis** 日常の中で

46. Keep A Clear Picture Of Your Love

Keep a clear picture in your mind of the love you feel for your partner. **Imagine what you like about them** in your mind, think about what their strengths are and the things you love them to do and say. Keep this picture even if it is not in your life right now. Have this clear picture of what you want in your future relationship as this helps to make it happen.

Love and happiness are usually part of that picture. Dream about your future with as much love and happiness as you can. Expect the best from your relationship and believe that **it can come true for you**.

あなたが手にしたいと思う理想の愛の形を、はっきりと思い浮かべましょう。
それが、理想を現実のものにする助けとなります。

....
imagine what you like about them　そのことについてあなたが好むことを思い描く　　it can come true for you　あなたにとって現実となる

47. Accept Differing Ideas And Beliefs

Do you and your partner have different ideas and beliefs? If you do then you are **like most people** in relationships. It is common in relationships to have beliefs and thoughts that are different from your partner.

It is easy to **get caught up with the thoughts and beliefs that you do not share** rather than with all the thoughts and beliefs that you do share—there are probably more of the latter than you think.

Accept that the differences between people add to the pleasure and richness of life. This is especially important in a relationship.

Look at the ideas and beliefs that you share and build on these. This way the relationship can grow and become stronger and this can lead to a healthy love.

誰でも違った考え方や価値観を持っています。
その違いにとらわれすぎてはいけません。
違いを受け入れることは、2人にとって重要なことです。

---

like most people 多くの人と同じように get caught up with the thoughts and beliefs that you do not share 自分とは違った考え方や価値観にとらわれる

48. Balance The Way You Talk

For a relationship to work, the way you talk to the other person needs to be mostly positive. Think and talk about positive things you see in them. If you keep telling them all the things they don't do well, it will break down the love between you and **the relationship can fall apart.**

Saying the same negative things over and over to your partner does not build a happy relationship.

Build a happy relationship by talking most of the time about the things that are working well; only talk about the things that are not working in a way that is kind and helpful. Take care to balance the way you talk with your partner.

相手にはポジティブに語りかけるようにしましょう。

---

the relationship can fall apart 2人の関係が壊れる　saying the same negative things over and over to your partner ネガティブなことを彼に言い続けること

49. Love Can Be All That You Hope For

All relationships need work and care to develop and grow. Love can be for you all that you hope but remember that love never stays the same, it changes all the time. Sometime it feels better, sometimes it feels like it isn't working. **As time goes by**, love will feel different as it grows and changes.

Have goals for your relationship and work with your partner to gain these. Practice the things needed to grow your love, such as talking and listening and showing your love for each other. You and your partner can live through these times, grow together and learn to love each other more and more as time passes.

> 2人の関係は、ともに育てていくことが必要です。
> 愛はいつも同じではありません。
> ときとともに変化していくものです。

---

as time goes by 時間がたつにつれて

SECTION 5

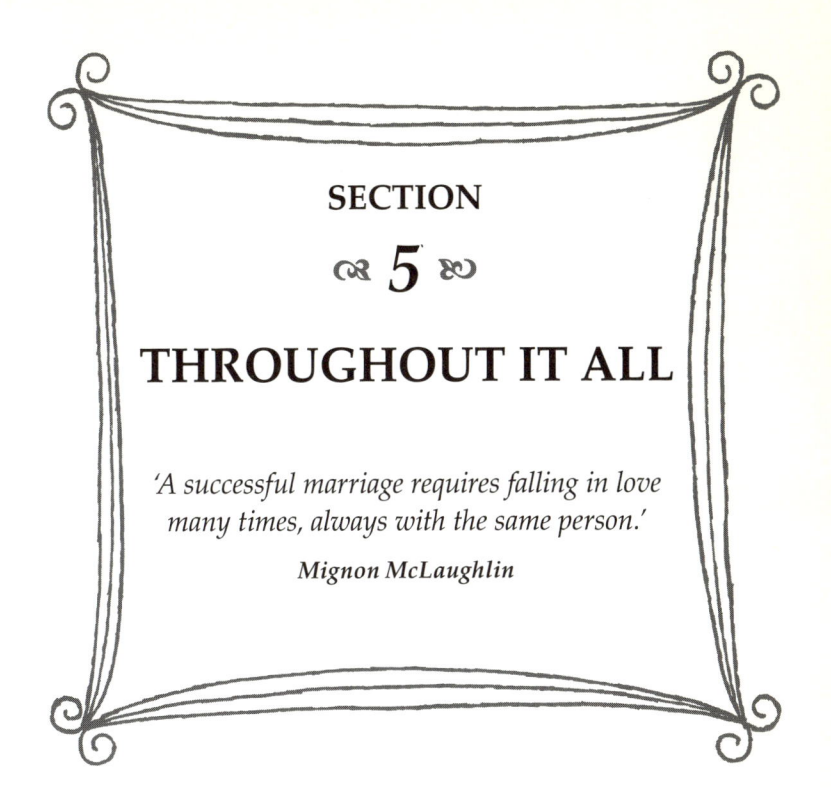

THROUGHOUT IT ALL

'A successful marriage requires falling in love many times, always with the same person.'

Mignon McLaughlin

50. Learn From Everything

Happy and positive events in your life make your soul strong and happy; negative and difficult events allow you to think about the way to do things and how you could do them differently next time. Negative and difficult events can also make your soul stronger.

You learn the most from events that are the most difficult for you. You learn the least from those that are least difficult.

When things happen to you that are positive or happy, you will enjoy them but do you think about them? Do you think about what caused them or have led them to you? Do you **think through** what you might learn from those events?

When things happen that make you unhappy or negative, you have an important choice. You can either be angry or you can think about what you might learn from them and how you might act differently in future.

**人は困難から、より多くを学ぶものです。
不幸な出来事にただ怒りをあらわにするか、そこから何かを学ぼうとするか。
あなたはどちらを選びますか。**

---

think through じっくりと考える

51. Move Past Anger

Everyone has events that happen to them that can leave them feeling **angry and upset**.

For example, **if you are treated badly at work** and you feel that you have done a good job, you have a choice. You might feel that it is not fair and dislike whoever has treated you badly and be angry. You might **feel like a victim** and ask yourself why the world is not kind to you, and feel angry. Or you might try to understand that sometimes things happen that are not nice, that whatever happened is past, is over and you should move on with your life.

There is no value in staying angry in your mind. Move on and be pleased with yourself for being positive. The choice is to be strong and learn, or to be sad and **pity yourself**. You make that choice.

よくないこともときには起こります。
ですがそれは過去のこと。終わったことなのです。
いつまでも怒りにとらわれたりせず、前に進むことです。

---

angry and upset 怒りやとまどい　　if you are treated badly at work もしあなたが会社で不当に扱われたら　　feel like a victim 被害者のように感じる　　pity yourself 自分を哀れむ

52. Teach Each Other

A loving relationship gives many great chances for two people who are close friends to understand each other better, and to understand themselves better. The reason for this is the amount of friendship and trust that can be created between two people in a close relationship. Trust may start with love but will grow with friendship and **sharing**. In sharing, there are times when you can learn new things about yourself as well as your partner.

New experiences give plenty of chances to learn and grow in your skills and knowledge. When you have a close relationship, you can help each other to understand the things that happen to you and **what lessons you might learn**. A close relationship gives you safety where you can learn.

With your partner, agree that you can talk to each other about your experiences and share in learning about what happens to each of you.

**相手への信頼は愛から生まれるかもしれませんが、
それを育てるのは友情と共有する思いです。**

....

sharing 共有する思い   what lessons you might learn あなたが学ぶであろう教訓

53. Dealing With Difficult Times

All relationships have difficulties at times. Sometimes difficulties mean that love is over and **the relationship is really at an end**. Other times difficulties will give you a chance to think carefully about what you want and whether your love is worth making changes to allow the relationship, and both of you, to grow.

If you feel unhappy in your relationship, think with some care about this question. Do you think and feel that you and your partner might be able to talk through each other's needs? Can you talk with each other, or does **your talking always lead to fights**? Can you try to work through differences?

If you can, then be prepared to listen as well as talk about your needs. Be prepared for change, but also be prepared for you and your partner to do things differently together and to work toward happiness again.

　　　2人の間に生じた問題は、関係を変化させるチャンスかもしれません。
　　　　そして2人を成長させるきっかけになるかもしれません。

---

dealing with difficult times 困難に対処する　the relationship is really at an end 2人の関係が本当に終わってしまう　your talking always lead to fights あなたの話のせいでいつもけんかになる

54. Moving Forward

When difficult times come up in a relationship it can be easy to either blame yourself for being the cause of the problem, or blame your partner. The truth is that one person alone is never responsible for a problem between two people; mostly, problems arise with each person **playing some part in making the problem**.

When there's a problem, first try to think of what part you have played in creating it. Be truthful but don't overstate your part. **If you blame yourself for everything** you will be too hard on yourself and take away from your **self-esteem**.

If you blame your partner for all of the problems in the relationship you will take away any chance of you both talking through the problem.

Be prepared to accept that you have probably added to whatever difficulties you are having in your relationship and accept that you can talk with your partner about these difficulties as a step **along the path to growing together**.

問題が起こったとき、原因はどちらか一方にあるのではなく、
何らかの形で両方にあるものです。自分を責めすぎるのも、
相手を責めすぎるのも、間違いです。

---

playing some part in making the problem　問題を起こすのに何らかの役割を演じている
if you blame yourself for everything　もしあなたがすべてを自分のせいにするなら
self-esteem　自尊心　　along the path to growing together　ともに成長する道を歩む

55. Don't Hold Back Your Love

Women have **an inbuilt gift** for caring and showing love, but some women hold back their love when they feel that their love and friendship are not returned the way they would like. If their boyfriend or partner is not showing his love in the way they want, they feel forgotten and unhappy. If this continues, **these feelings can take over** and turn into dislike and anger.

It is important to love openly and **not close down your love**, even if you feel you are not receiving the love you want. Talk with your partner about how you feel and explain how you would like to be treated. This shows care for yourself and the long-term relationship.

> あなたの思ったように愛情や友情が示されなかったとしても、
> あなたの気持ちを抑え込んではいけません。
> 愛することをやめてはいけません。

---

hold back your love 気持ちを抑える　　an inbuilt gift 天賦の才能　　these feelings can take over そういった気持ちが心を占めて　　not close down your love 愛することをやめない

56. Trying To Please Everyone Doesn't Work

Everyone is busy in their work and women can **find it hard to please everyone** in their lives. Doing your work well, having a happy relationship, relaxing and spending time with friends and family are hard to do all at once. Sometimes all this can lead to stress.

You cannot please everyone. It is best to have some very clear thoughts about what you want for yourself and follow these, rather than trying to be all things to everyone and trying to make everyone happy. Remember to listen to your own beliefs and values and follow these. **Work out what you believe in** and follow that every day. If you do this you will be less stressed and a happier, more honest person.

すべての人を満足させることなどできません。
あなたにとって本当に必要な人は誰なのか、心の声に耳を傾けるのです。

---

find it hard to please everyone 皆を満足させるのは困難であると気づく　　work out what you believe in あなたが信じるものに精力を傾ける

57. No-one Stays The Same

It's easy to think that your partner will stay the same as he was when you first met. Change always happens in every relationship, at different times and **at different stages of the relationship**. Adapting to change is something you need to do as the relationship grows. **Adapting to change** means being able to see the changes that are happening around you and keeping an open mind to doing things differently.

Relationships usually start with lots of things that you both like about each other. It's easy to forget why you liked each other at first when things change in your life. Every day, try to remember the good things about the other person and tell them about these things.

This helps to **look after the relationship in a very special way**.

変わらない人などいません。変化していくことは
2人の関係を成長させる上でとても大切なことなのです。

---

at different stages of the relationship つき合いのさまざまな段階で　　adapting to change 変化に順応する　　look after the relationship in a very special way 2人の関係を特別に大切なものにする

58. Stay Connected To Your Feelings

Throughout your relationship stay connected to your feelings. Take notice and think about your feelings without being hurt or upset.

Your feelings will always help you to understand what is happening in your world and in your relationship. They are very useful in telling you if something is or isn't right. They can connect you to what is happening for you and what is happening around you.

Sit gently with these feelings and carefully listen to them. Sometimes you will decide to act upon them, sometimes you will just notice them and feel kindness to yourself for feeling them and then let them go.

　　自分の気持ちにもっと耳を傾けましょう。そしてその心の声に従うのです。
　　　　心の声は、あなたに警告を与えてくれたり、
　　　　状況を的確に判断してくれたりするものです。

---

stay connected to your feelings 自分の心の声に常に耳を傾ける

59. When You Decide To Act On Your Feelings

When you decide that you want to do something about how you feel, ask questions about what you think is happening and check with your partner about how you can go forward together with a better understanding of each other.

But always remember to **be true to yourself**. Act on what is true for you and on what you believe is right for you. Be yourself and act calmly and clearly with your partner. Expressing your values can help you to be more in control and less emotional.

'It doesn't work for me in my relationship if I lose who I am and don't notice my values, because I then **end up hating** the other person because I am not who I really am with them.'

Mary

Be true to yourself always.

自分に正直でいましょう。自分の価値観をしっかり持っていれば、感情的でない落ち着いた行動がとれるようになるはずです。

---

be true to yourself 自分に正直でいる　　**end up hating** 結局は嫌いになる

60. When You Think Too Much

Sally is a woman who worries too much. She said, 'I really worry about small things that happen. Sometimes these things have happened three days ago and I am still worrying about them. If my boyfriend does something that I don't like, I worry about it endlessly.'

Sally makes small thing into big things often. Something small becomes something big because she has thought too much about it for three days.

Do you think too much about the past and then that becomes a worry? Are you an **over-worrier**? Some people think about something that happened yesterday and this turns to worry about what they said or didn't say, or could have said to their partner.

The key is to let go of thoughts about the past and live in present time. Just **remind yourself what you are doing now**. You may be sitting in a chair or in a train or at work or sitting at home; wherever you are right now is important. Try to bring yourself back to what is happening at this moment.

Thinking about the past and trying to change something that has already passed is a very hard way to treat yourself. No one can change the past. **Let go of what you said or did yesterday** and look at where and what you are doing right now.

誰であっても過去を変えることはできません。
過去について思い悩んでも、何も解決されません。それよりも大切なのは、
あなたの「今」です。今を生きることを考えるのです。

---

over-worrier とても心配性の人　　remind yourself what you are doing now 今していることを自分に言い聞かせる　　let go of what you said or did yesterday あなたが昨日言ったことやしたことは忘れましょう

61. Don't Try To Change The Other Person

Many people start a relationship thinking they can fix someone else or make another person better in a way they want them to be. This does not work. Don't ever believe that asking someone to change will make them change; it won't. If someone else is ready to change, they will change because they want to, not because someone else has asked them to do it.

People do not change because you ask them to. People change because their life is such that they have to change because what they are doing is so **uncomfortable** or hurtful to them that they have to find a better way to do it.

Love and accept your partner. Change the things about yourself you can change and love and **accept them as they are**.

相手を変えようという試みは、決して成功しません。
相手を変えようとするのではなく、
あるがままの彼を愛せるように、自分を変えるのです。

---

uncomfortable 不快な　　accept them as they are あるがままの相手を受け入れる

62. Don't Put Others Before Yourself

Do you **care for yourself** well, or do you see the other person's needs as more important than your own? When you care for yourself and begin from strength you will have more energy to care for another person in a relationship. Caring for yourself well is strength, not weakness.

Just because you could do so much for another person doesn't mean you should. You must keep some energy for yourself. Sometimes caring for yourself means saying 'No' to someone you love.

'Your first love needs to be of self. Without that you have very little to give.'

Jenny

自分を大切にすることは、弱さのあらわれではありません。
自分を愛することができて初めて、他人を思いやることができるのです。

---

put others before yourself 自分よりも他人を優先する　　care for yourself 自分を大切にする

63. Have Energy For Yourself

Living a busy life and having so many different areas of your life that need your time can **break down your energy**. If you feel like your energy is getting low, here are some things you can do to keep good strong energy for yourself:

- Find time to be by yourself, for yourself.
- Say, 'No' if you have too much to do.
- Ask for help if and when you need it.
- Make a list of all the good things about yourself and read it every day for a month.
- Work out something you enjoy doing and make time to do it every day, even if just for half an hour.
- Have more sleep or relaxation.

Any of these things will help you to keep strong positive energy for yourself.

　　　毎日忙しくしていると、エネルギーが切れてしまうことがあります。
　　　そんなときには、積極的に充電する時間や機会を持ちましょう。

....
break down your energy あなたのエネルギーを損なう

64. Distance Yourself From Friends You Cannot Trust

If you feel that a friend is not true or honest with you or does not share your values, talk with them first and try to **clear things up between you.** If they continue to be **dishonest and not supportive of your values**, you can make the decision not to spend time with them. You can do this quietly without making trouble.

If you hold on to a friendship when you cannot trust that friend, you are likely to **bring harm and pain to yourself.** You may think that you should accept them as they are and give them another chance, but to do so will **lessen your self-esteem** and can invite trouble and hard times to you.

If they are being dishonest or your trust and friendship is not returned, your spirit will feel that the relationship is not fair to you. Your self-esteem will be lessened. Your friendship with others who are truer to you may also be lessened.

You need to distance yourself from others who are not trustworthy.

友人があなたにとって信用できない態度を取り続けるなら、
勇気を持って距離を置くことです。
つき合い続けると、あなた自身がすり減ってしまいます。

....

clear things up between you　互いの間の問題を解決する　　dishonest and not supportive of your values　誠意がなく、あなたの価値観に対して助けとならない　　bring harm and pain to yourself　あなたに悪影響と苦痛をもたらす　　lessen your self-esteem　あなたの自尊心を損なう

65. Be Careful How People Talk To You

Have you ever walked away from a friend and felt badly? Felt like something the other person did or said wasn't nice or didn't feel right? Sometimes friendships change and **your friends may not have your best interests at heart**. They may feel jealous of what you have.

Trust that feeling of something not being right if you feel it about a friend. Sometimes you have to **let go of a past friendship** because it is not healthy for you anymore.

'I loved my school friend Sak, but she was so jealous of my life with my boyfriend and my job. We just didn't have any fun together. I miss her but I had to stop seeing her as it was poisoning my life. It was just not nice to be with her any more, she was becoming so **cruel**.'

Lucy

友情も変化することがあります。
もし友人があなたのことを思っていないと分かったなら、
勇気を持って、過去の友情を手放しましょう。

---

your friends may not have your best interests at heart 友人は、本当はあなたのためを思っていないかもしれない　　**let go of a past friendship** 過去の友情を手放す　　**cruel** 残酷な

SECTION 6

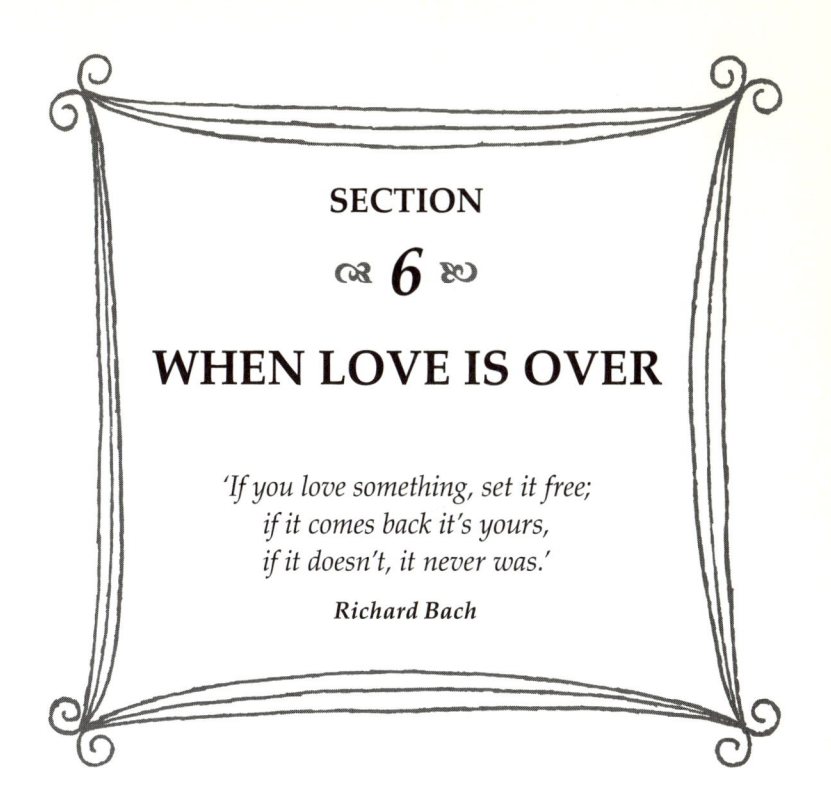

WHEN LOVE IS OVER

*'If you love something, set it free;
if it comes back it's yours,
if it doesn't, it never was.'*

Richard Bach

66. Freedom Of Choice

There may come a time when you feel you have done everything you can in a relationship and it just does not seem to be working.

If you have put the time and effort into your relationship and done everything you can to make it work, if your partner does not want to change and if you are always unhappy, you have three choices.

1. You can choose to change your thoughts about what you want from your partner and the relationship.
2. You can accept who and what your partner is.
3. You can **leave the relationship.**

If you are worried about your relationship, give careful thought to these three choices.

あらゆる努力をしても、2人の関係がうまくいかなくなったとしたら、じっくりと考えることが必要です。

---

leave the relationship つき合いを解消する

67. Know When To Leave

In a new relationship, everyone hopes that their love will grow and that both of you will become stronger together, happily growing as a loving couple. This doesn't always happen.

While many relationships do grow, some do not. This is sad, but true. How do you know when a relationship is over? Your heart will tell you and **your intuition will tell you**. You may feel sad, the pleasure of seeing your partner may go, you may feel doubt and pain and you may feel that the love between you is over.

If you feel these feelings, think very carefully about whether you should stay in the relationship or end it. If you stay in an unhappy relationship, you do not look after your best interests. Long-lasting sadness will hurt you and make it hard for you to be happy again in the future.

If your partner is not able to talk with you honestly about the problems and difficulties that you are feeling, you should take care of yourself and end the relationship.

Know when to leave. Work out how to tell your partner it's over and make your plans to leave.

不幸な関係を続けていると、あなた自身が傷つくだけでなく、将来の幸せをも見失うことになってしまいます。

---

your intuition will tell you　直感があなたに語りかける

68. Stop Blaming

Many people blame and judge the person they have loved for all the bad things that have happened in their lives. They do not stop to think that they have added something to these events in some way.

Everyone has more control of their lives than they think they have. It can be very healing to accept that your thoughts and actions may have made your life what it is right now.

Don't blame the person you love or have loved in the past for what has or hasn't worked for you in your life. Accept the things you and the other person have done in the past and **move on**. Don't think over and over about the past.

Fix the things you are able to fix and **let go of the past**. Make changes for the future by the way you think and act now. This will create the best possible future for you and your partner and your life will become much more positive.

> 今も愛している人や、かつて愛した人を責めるのはやめましょう。
> 過去を手放し、未来に向けて気持ちを切り替えるのです。

---

stop blaming 責めるのをやめにする　　move on 前に進む　　let go of the past 過去を手放す

69. When Things Are Finally Over

When a relationship is over and you accept that **it cannot be brought back to life**, there is pain, often there is blame, and sometimes a woman will blame herself for not doing enough to keep the relationship **in good health**.

Time will heal this pain.

If you are blaming your former partner for the failure of the relationship, the sooner you let go of this blame the better it will be for you. Blame is never useful; it does nothing except keep the pain of what went wrong alive in you.

Everyone could find things they could have done better, so forgive yourself for not being better or different in the past and decide to be better in the future. Learn from your mistakes; mistakes help you to make better decisions next time.

As quickly as you are able, put your past relationship behind you. Think about your future and how you are looking forward to the new and exciting things that will come into your life.

> もう自分を責めるのはやめましょう。
> もっとうまくできたはずだと思うなら、
> その経験を未来に生かすのです。

---

it cannot be brought back to life 元に戻すことはできない　　in good health よい状態に

70. The Steps Of Grief

When a relationship is over, don't be surprised if you feel it quite deeply. When you experience loss in a relationship it is easy to **get lost in grief and pain**. There are five stages of grief and it is sometimes hard to move from one stage to the other.

Denial: 'This can't be happening to me,' not yet crying or letting go, not accepting what has happened.

Anger: 'Why me?' feelings of wanting to fight back or hurt the other person, blaming them for leaving you.

Making a deal: Trying to make deals with the person who is leaving or God, to stop or change what has happened.

Sadness: **An overwhelming feeling of loss**, hurt, feeling sorry for yourself. Feeling lack of control, sad and hopeless.

Acceptance: Accepting the loss of the relationship. Finding the good that can come out of the pain of loss, your goals turn toward the future and you remember the past with fond memories of the other person.

Being aware of where you are on this journey helps in moving forward. You won't feel what you are feeling now forever.

悲しみは、「否定、怒り、取引、悲しみ、受容」という5つのステップを踏みます。
自分が今どの段階にあるか考えてみましょう。
悲しみは、永遠に続くものではないのです。

---

get lost in grief and pain 悲しみと苦しみで自分を見失う　　making a deal 取引をする
an overwhelming feeling of loss どうしようもない喪失感

71. Look To The Future With Hope

Understand that when a relationship is over you will **survive and go on with your life**. Even if you cannot believe that just now, you will heal. Even if you do not believe this at the time, know that it will become true for you at some time in the future. To feel pain after loss is normal. It proves that you are alive and that you are human.

Don't stop living your life; become stronger, become hopeful that one day you will find love and happiness again. Your experience has added something to your life and will help you to look at things with more wisdom next time. In time, something good always comes from something hurtful.

生きることをあきらめないことです。
その経験は次に生かされるのですから。
つらいことの後には必ずいいことがやってくるものです。

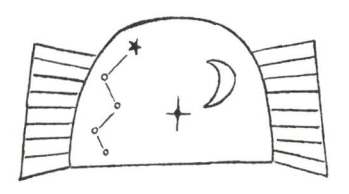

---

survive and go on with your life なんとか人生を続けていく

72. Try Something New

When you are ready to move forward, try doing something new or different in your life. Focus your mind on learning something new; perhaps **a musical instrument**, a new skill, new sport or interest. Try something you always wanted to do but never got around to doing.

'When I broke up with my boyfriend I started to play tennis. I always wanted to try this and never thought I had the time to spend on it. I really enjoyed it and found that I met many people at the practice sessions. It really opened up my life for me again.'

Sook

Breaking up with someone, whether after a month or a lifetime, can bring new chances and hope for you.

前に進む準備ができたなら、何か新しいことを始めてみましょう。
きっと新しいチャンスや希望を生むきっかけになることでしょう。

....

a musical instrument 楽器

73. Do Something Kind For Someone Else

Taking the focus from yourself and thinking about others and how you can be kind to them allows your body to heal and to get better.

Think about someone you know well or not so well and do something nice for them today. You can do it so that they know about it and can thank you or you can do it without them knowing **where the good deed came from**.

Here are some suggestions about how you can be kind to others:

- Treat everyone you know as if they are part of your family.
- Take some special treats to work/school and share them with others.
- Let the person in the line who is in a hurry be served before you.
- Open the door for someone else and smile as you do it.
- Clean out all your old clothes and give them away to people who need them.
- Help someone who is younger than you to do something that is difficult.
- Tell your best friend **you appreciate her or him**.

....
where the good deed came from その親切な行いがどこからきたのか you appreciate her or him 彼女や彼に感謝している

- Next time someone speaks to you, listen carefully to their every word.

- Offer your services to do something for someone for free.

Being kind to others is also **a gentle reminder** for you to be kind to yourself. Do some of the kind things from the list above for yourself; you are worthy of feeling good about yourself.

人にやさしくしてみましょう。
人へのやさしさは、実は自分を癒やすことにつながっています。

---

a gentle reminder　穏やかな合図

SECTION

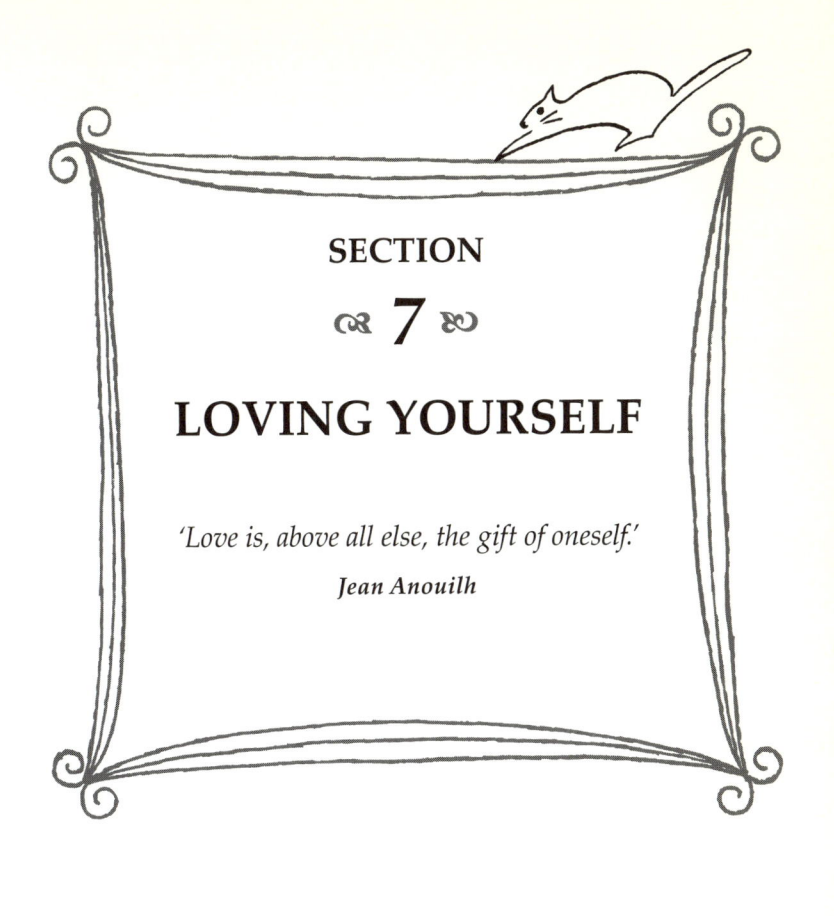

✃ 7 ✃

LOVING YOURSELF

'Love is, above all else, the gift of oneself.'
Jean Anouilh

74. How You See Yourself

Are you kind to yourself when you think about your body, or are you unkind to yourself about your body and **how you look**?

Do you like the way you look or do you think you should be taller or prettier or thinner or have a different—looking body? If you don't like yourself now because of the way you look, you may not like yourself any better if you were able to change.

Learn to like all the good things about yourself, now. Think about all the things about yourself that you like and learn to like yourself as you are right now.

Change what you can change, but accept who and what you are right now. If you do want to change something about yourself, start with something you can change like your weight, hair style or color, general look, or **eating habits**. Set small goals for the things you can change, as well as liking yourself as you are right now.

もし外見が理由で自分を好きになれないのなら、
自分を好きになれる日はこれから先もおとずれないでしょう。
まず今の自分を受け入れるのです。
そして、実現可能な小さな目標を立て実行していくのです。

---

how you look 外見　　eating habits 食生活

75. Don't Compare Yourself With Others

The media often write about the wealth and beauty of rock stars and movie stars, sports people and authors. These people have become people we **look up to**. Papers and websites are often full of stories and pictures about these 'perfect' people with 'perfect' bodies and lives. Do you really believe all these stories?

It is too easy for women to feel like failures when they **measure themselves against famous people**.

You may also think that the people you know, your friends and people you work with, are more beautiful or smarter than you.

You are a special person; no one is like you. Whatever you are right now is special. You must learn to accept and like yourself rather than being unkind to yourself by measuring yourself against other people.

自分を他人と比べるのは、やめましょう。
芸能人や友人と比べてよいことなど何もありません。
あなたは特別な存在なのです。どこにもあなたのような人はいないのです。

....
don't compare yourself with others 自分を他人と比べない　　look up to あこがれる
measure themselves against famous people 有名人と自分を比べる

76. Be Positive About Yourself

It is healthy to think and feel positive about yourself. Here are some things you can do to feel positive about yourself:

- Accept that you are not perfect and you never will be.
- Look at the positive, the many things that are good about you.
- Be grateful for the good things already in your life.
- Don't think about the future too much.
- Have a dream for the future, but live now.
- Relax, **let go of worry**.
- Care for yourself and others.
- Meet people and make friends.

Learn to laugh more and play; have fun with your partner and friends.

自分に対してポジティブに感じることはよいことです。
彼や友人とともに、笑い、遊び、大いに楽しむのです。

---

let go of worry 不安を取り除く

77. Mistakes Are Great

Everyone makes choices about their lives that sometimes don't **work out** for them. Everyone makes mistakes every day. When you make a mistake, the most important thing is not to be too unkind to yourself. Learn from these mistakes, and use every thing that happens to you as **a learning point**.

Welcome mistakes in your life. When you know about a mistake and accept that you have made it you can learn from it. Forgive yourself about making mistakes and learn what to do and what not to do next time.

That's the gift a mistake can give you—the gift of learning about yourself and about what you could do better and more wisely next time.

誰でも毎日のように間違いを犯します。
ですがそのことで自分を責めすぎてはいけません。
私たちはそこから次への教訓を学べるのです。

---

work out うまくいく　　**a learning point** 学びの場

78. Don't Beat Yourself Up About Mistakes

What do you say to yourself when you make a mistake? Is it mostly good and positive, as it would be if you were talking to a friend? Or is what you say to yourself negative and hurtful?

Learning to love yourself when you make mistakes is one of the most important things you will ever do. Everyone makes mistakes; this is how you really learn about yourself and the world. Mistakes can make you more **understanding** and teach you to be a better person. Most people learn and grow through making mistakes and then they change what they do next time.

Be open to learn from mistakes so you may learn and grow as a person.

失敗したときにも、自分自身にやさしくしてあげましょう。
失敗しない人などいません。
私たちは失敗から学び、成長していくのです。

---

understanding 寛大な　　**be open to learn from mistakes** 心を広く持ち失敗から学ぶ

79. Be Careful About Who You Spend Time With

Do people around you speak badly about themselves or about others when you are with them? Do they say unpleasant things about what they or others look like or how or what they eat?

Being around people like this can make you feel bad. If your friends don't think the same way you think or the way you want to think, you can change who you spend time with.

It may not be easy to spend less time with people you are used to being with, but if they don't support the way you think and feel about yourself and your body, then **for your own health and well being** it may be better for you not to be with them.

**いつも一緒にいる人があなたを嫌な気持ちにさせるなら、
相手を変えることです。それはあなたの心と体の健康のためになります。**

....
for your own health and well being あなたの心と体の健康のため

80. Have A Healthy Body

It is not unusual to hear a teenager and her mother speak the same way about food and exercise because they have the same beliefs about food and exercise.

The same can be said about you and your friends. The way you and others speak and feel about your body has an impact on your attitude toward how you feel and look. Find the company of friends who have a healthy attitude toward their bodies and how they look after and care for them.

It is easy to reflect the values and beliefs of those you spend time with. Be with people who **have a healthy relationship** with food and their body. For just as you take good things from what you eat, you also take the views, whether good or bad, of those you spend time with.

食べるものに意識を向け、自分の体を大切にしている友人を持ちましょう。
彼らと過ごすことで、あなたの感じ方やものの見方に、
よい影響がもたらされるでしょう。

---

have a healthy relationship よい関係を持つ

81. Don't Be Competitive With Friends

Some people want to be better than their friends in all areas of their lives. They are **competitive** in sports, work, how many friends they have, how much money they spend or the way they look. **They compete with their friends** to be better than them rather than enjoy them.

Men mainly try to be better than each other in sport and work. Women try to be better than other women more quietly with body shape, body size and beauty.

Try to spend time with people who are not trying to be better than you. Find people who have good, balanced values and who like you the way you are.

> 自分が友人より優れていないとおさまらないという人がいます。
> そういう人とはつき合わないことです。
> あなたのあるがままを受け入れてくれる友人を見つけましょう。

---

competitive 負けず嫌いの　　they compete with their friends 彼らは友人と張り合う

82. Move Your Body

Exercise is a positive way to help your body to feel good. Find what exercises you like and that help make you feel good about yourself.

Exercise can be simple. Walk some of the distance to work, take the time to get off your bus or train one stop earlier on your journey and walk the rest of the way. This is a small but positive way to exercise your body.

Walk up the stairs instead of using the elevator. Ride a bike or walk to work or to the shops instead of going by car, bus or train. Try **yoga** for 30 minutes a day; this is simple exercise that is very good for you. **Practice breathing well.**

Exercise allows your body to feel well and happy.

心と体を健康に保つためにエクササイズをしましょう。
一駅前でおりて歩く、エレベーターでなく階段を使うなど、
簡単なものでよいのです。

---

yoga ヨガ　**Practice breathing well.** よい呼吸法を練習しましょう。

83. Relax

Relaxing is a big part of caring for your body. There are other ways to relax than reading and watching television. Relaxation can be about taking some time out from actively doing things all the time.

You can relax and lessen stress by doing the following:

- Lie down and relax your body.
- Close your eyes.
- **Let go of any stress.**
- **Uncross your arms and legs.**
- Take some deep breaths, hold each breath for a couple of seconds and let it go.
- Allow your body to relax.
- Think about each part of your body in turn and let go of any stress you may feel in that part of your body.
- Try not to think thoughts that worry or stress you.
- **Let your body feel calm.**
- Enjoy this feeling.

Try to stay that way for at least five minutes. Do this once or twice every day.

リラックスして体をいたわりましょう。
1日に一度か二度、そのための時間を持つことです。

....

Let go of any stress. ストレスを解放させましょう   **Uncross your arms and legs.** 腕や足を組むのをやめましょう。   **Let your body feel calm.** 体を落ち着かせましょう。

84. Have Fun

When you relax your body you feel good about yourself. Having fun is another way to relax and enjoy yourself. This can mean doing good things like:

- Cook the food you like.
- Take a holiday.
- Clean your home and **make it special**.
- Have nice things around you.
- Get some flowers for your home.
- Go to the movies.
- Play the music you love.
- Be kind to yourself every day.
- Read, draw, write, play, laugh and walk more.

'I love to draw pictures of trees and flowers. I'm not much good at it, but it's so **unlike what I do** in my job all day, every day. This is my way to let go and have fun.'

Tina

What do you enjoy doing? What helps you to **feel lighter** and happier? How could you do more of this in your life?

積極的に楽しいことをして、リラックスしましょう。
心が軽くなり、楽しめることは何でしょうか?

....

make it special 特別なものにする　　**unlike what I do** やっていることと違うこと　　**feel lighter** 心が軽くなる

85. Sit Well And Stand Tall

Almost everyone uses a computer these days; emails and the Internet have made computers a big part of our lives. Also, your computer is often used as part of your study or work or leisure time. This can have a poor effect on the way you sit and the way you stand. **Leaning over a computer** can cause **stress and discomfort.** When you are at the computer, remember to sit up straight and relax your shoulders and place your feet flat on the floor; don't cross your legs.

It's the same with standing. Many people stand in their work or have to stand for a long time during the day. Stand up straight and tall as it is important for **good health and wellness.**

Both sitting well and standing straight are good for your breathing too.

コンピューターの前に座りっぱなしになっていませんか。
背筋を伸ばしてまっすぐ立っていますか。
正しく座り、立つことは、あなたの呼吸も楽にします。

....

leaning over a computer　コンピューターに向かって前のめりになる　　stress and discomfort　ストレスと不快感　　good health and wellness　健やかな心と体

86. Learn To Breathe Correctly

Breathing is easy; you don't have to think about it, it just happens. How do you breathe most of the time? Long deep breaths or short sharp breaths, or **somewhere in between**?

Most of us breathe short breaths most of the time, but breathing like this all the time does not look after your body as well as breathing deeply does. When you breathe deeply it centers your body and helps you to relax.

If you want to check how you are breathing do the following;

- Lie down. Put a book on your **stomach** and another book on your **chest**.

- Take a deep breath.

- If the book on your stomach rises higher than the one on your chest you are breathing as deeply as you could.

Every day, be more aware of how you breathe, especially when you are stressed or worried. Breathing deeply almost always **calms your body and your mind**.

呼吸に意識を向けるようにしましょう。
深い呼吸はあなたの体や心を落ち着かせます。

---

somewhere in between　その中間くらい　　stomach　腹部　　chest　胸部　　calms your body and your mind　体と心を落ち着かせる

87. Time For Yourself

Do you make time for yourself? Do you have times where you do things just for you?

Our work culture **has placed a high value on paid work**. Everyone works longer hours at their everyday jobs so it may not feel natural to spend time for yourself by yourself. Some people make their relaxation time **as busy as a work day**. They fit in so much that they never seem to stop doing things, either at work or in their own time.

Allow quiet time for yourself; it is very healthy to treat yourself in this way.

自分だけの時間を持っていますか。
自分だけの静かなひとときを確保することは、とても大切なことなのです。

---

has placed a high value on paid work　お金になる仕事を価値あるものとしてきた
as busy as a work day　仕事の日と同じくらい忙しく

88. Do You Get Too Stressed?

Do you sometimes **feel stressed out**? Do you worry about things in your life that you can do nothing about? Do you feel negative sometimes? Or worry about work, family and friends? Are you afraid to meet new people sometimes? Do you sometimes feel worried about the future?

If any of these things happen to you there is something you can do to help yourself. Try to think about the good things that happen around you, not just the negative things. Do one small thing at a time and be happy to do that.

Relax your thinking as well as your body.

Talk to someone you trust about your feelings and fears or **write a journal or a diary** about how you feel. Think most about the present, not the past or the future. You may like to exercise more, or walk every day. These are all good ways to start feeling good about yourself.

ストレスに押しつぶされていませんか。
過去や未来のことを考えるのではなく、今に思いを巡らしましょう。

---

feel stressed out　ストレスを感じている　　write a journal or a diary　日記を書く

89. Nurture A Healthy Self-image

Your self-image is how you see yourself. This is different from how you feel about yourself, which is self-esteem. Is your self-view real about the whole of you—your skills at work, how you look, your relationship skills, your energy, your goals, your friendliness and your **compassion**?

To help you **develop a realistic self-image**, write two lists. Write one with your strengths (things you are good at) and one with your weaknesses (things you would like to change or do better).

When you start, the weaknesses list is likely to be longer than the strengths. When you really think about yourself you will be surprised to find that there are so many strengths, so many good things about you. Don't overlook things you might think are small; it is strength to be able to do your work well, keep your home in good order, to be a good friend to someone, to be kind to a pet, to tell the truth.

Think about these strengths every day as this builds a healthy and realistic self-image that will help you to feel good about yourself.

よいセルフイメージを持ちましょう。
自分の長所は何かを考えるよう心がけましょう。
リストアップしていくと、たくさんの長所に気づくはずです。

---

nurture a healty self-image 健全なセルフイメージを育む　　compassion 思いやり
develop a realistic self-image　現実的なセルフイメージを構築する

90. Build Your Self-esteem

It's important to feel good and to be clear and strong about your skills and about what you can do.

No one is perfect, but **you are mostly capable**. Remember that you have good skills in your work, you have some relationship skills and you can talk clearly, listen and **achieve your goals**. You may not fit the popular magazine pictures for size, figure, dress and the bag you carry, but you can still dress well, or buy nice things. While there may be a few things you would like to change about yourself, you are probably more OK **than you think you are**.

When you think about yourself, do you like yourself? Do you see yourself as positively as you really are? Do you feel mostly good about yourself? Do you have good self-esteem? Or do you talk badly to yourself about **those few things you might like to improve about yourself**?

To help with this, think about your strengths, the things you are good at. Think about the things you do well each day rather than talking badly to yourself about any small things you could have done better.

　　自分に自信を持つことはとても大切です。完璧な人などいないのですから。
　　できないことに目を向けるのではなく、自分ができていることを見つめるのです。

---

self-esteem 自尊心　　you are mostly capable あなたはだいたいできている　　achieve your goals 目標を達成する　　than you think you are あなたが思う自分より　　those few things you might lilke to improve about yourself そうした自分について改善したいと思うこと

91. Take Control

The things you hear from others, the words you speak to others and the words you speak to yourself can all **make a difference to you**, to your life and your thoughts.

If you hear negative things all the time, you are more likely to become negative in your thinking and your actions. If you often say hard or unkind things about others, you are likely to become hard and unkind in your own heart.

You can control your own thoughts and stop negative thinking. You also can choose to control how people talk to you. If people around you often say negative or unpleasant things, you can either ask them to change what they are talking about or not listen to them. You will be a stronger and better person if you do this.

ネガティブな言葉とは距離を保ちましょう。
それはあなたの考え方や行動に影響を及ぼします。

---

make a difference to you あなたに影響を及ぼす

92. Don't Shoot The Messenger!

When someone tells you something, there are two separate parts to the message you hear. The first part is what is said and the second part is what you think and feel at the time about the person who brings you the message.

There is a saying, 'Don't shoot the messenger.' This saying comes from stories told in the history of war. **When bad news was delivered**, the general would have the messenger shot so that the soldiers would not find out about this bad news.

If you do not like what is in the message, try not to be angry about it, try not to put **all your attention** on the person giving it. It is very important not to focus only on the person who brings the message. As the saying goes, 'Don't shoot the messenger.' They are not the problem.

Think about what you can learn from each message. Is there some part of what is said that you should think about? Sometimes the message isn't about you at all, or it may be wrong. It may show the feelings of the person who brings the message, rather than be something about you.

Try to think about what information could be useful for you, and leave the rest alone. But **in any case**, don't shoot the messenger!

あなたが望まないことを言った人を恨んではいけません。
言われた内容と、言った人とを切り離して考えることが必要です。

'Don't shoot the messenger'「メッセンジャーを撃つな」　when bad news was delivered 悪いニュースが伝えられると　all your attention あなたのすべての関心
in any case どんな場合でも

93. Learn To Like Yourself

Many women think that the love of a man will make them happy. Some women fear being alone because they see it as **shameful**. The truth of it is that women are very strong and can be happy living on their own. When you learn to live with yourself and like yourself you truly become strong.

It is possible to be just as alone when you are with someone in a relationship as when you are not with someone; when you are with someone who is making you unhappy you can feel very alone.

Learn to like yourself because this **builds good feelings** about yourself and helps you to feel good no matter who is or isn't in your life.

1人で幸せでいられる女性は、本当に強い女性です。
それはパートナーがいる、いないに関係ないことなのです。

---

shameful 恥ずかしい   builds good feelings よい感情を育む

94. When You Are On Your Own You Can Learn And Grow

It's OK if you are alone at the moment, if you are not in a relationship. Whether it is for a short time or a lifetime, it can **provide a great space for you to learn and grow**.

Being **on your own** for some time may well be just the right thing for you to give you the chance to think about what you really want and who you really are. If you have been hurt before, being on your own can heal you and help you to feel strong again.

Trust yourself if you are on your own and you will learn and grow as a person.

自分を見つめるために1人でいることは正しいことです。
それはあなたに、人間としての成長をもたらす力となります。

---

provide a great space for you to learn and grow 学び成長する機会を与える
on your own 自分1人で

95. Connect With Yourself

Take time to **nurture yourself. Get in touch with your inner self,** your inner wisdom.

Being still is a great way to get in touch with the real you. When you stop thinking and just sit and **let your mind drift,** you create a space for your inner self to breathe, creating a rich inner life, a life that isn't about other people and action, just about you and your inner true self. Each person has their own way of connecting with this inner part of themselves. Try your own way to find some space and time to stop and **let go of everyday life.**

'When I sit still and stop thinking, there is this other part of me who is just kind of happy and **at ease with myself,** just sitting doing nothing. This is my inner self. I feel better about myself when I make time to sit quietly and let go of my mind trying to make sense of everything all the time. When I make time to do that I am a much happier person and much less stressed.'

Kylie

内なる自分と触れ合う時間を持ちましょう。
考えるのをやめて、静かに座り、心を解放するのです。

---

connect with yourself 自分とつながる　　nurture yourself 自分を成長させる
get in touch with your inner self 内なる自分と交信する　　let your mind drift あなたの心を漂わせる　　let go of everyday life 日常を忘れる　　at ease with myself 自分だけでリラックスして

96. Your Needs Are Important

Make time in your diary each week just for you. You can do anything you want with this time as long as you keep that time for yourself. Unless you live away from everything, there is usually some sort of noise going on around you, even if it is just **the quiet hum of a computer**. Trains, cars, people, television and loud music all make the world around you a busy place to be.

Time alone is a caring and very supporting thing to do for yourself. Start with two minutes a day and build this up to a longer time.

It is just as important to make this time whether you are a student, in paid work or not; making time for yourself **improves your sense of real value and self worth**. When you spend time by yourself your values will become clearer and **more certain**. Time alone will help you to be clear about your values and what you want in your life.

自分のためだけに使う時間を確保しましょう。
騒がしい日常から離れて過ごすことで、
本当の価値観や自尊心が養われるようになるのです。

---

the quiet hum of a computer　コンピューターの小さなモーター音　　improves your sense of real value and self worth　あなたの真の価値観や自尊心を向上させる　　more certain　より確かに

97. Balance Your Needs

It is easy to care about other people's needs and forget about your own needs. Do you care too much about what other people suggest you do or ask you to do, and not enough about your own needs?

Some women believe their value is about doing things for other people to please them or to make them like you.

Sometimes women find it easier to let go of the time they have **set aside** for themselves because it is easier to do this than tell someone else they are going to keep this time for themselves. Sometimes it seems easier to let other people's needs be more important than your own; easier to **give in** to someone else's needs than your own.

When you make time for yourself you will help to keep your life in balance.

  人のことばかりを優先して、自分のことを後回しにしていませんか。
  自分の時間を大切にすると、人生がバランスのとれたものになっていきます。

---

set aside とっておく **give in** 譲る

98. Your Best Friend

If you were married to you, how long would you stay married? You need to be mostly positive to keep a relationship with someone else strong, but do you know how to keep a happy and positive relationship with yourself?

Everyone knows that to be healthy they need to look after themselves. You can care for yourself in **many physical ways.** But how do you care for yourself in your thoughts and feelings? Are you kind to yourself in the way that you think about yourself? Do you think kind, loving thoughts about yourself? Do you like yourself? Are you having any fun yet?

Doing things to care for yourself is a positive habit. Being kind to one's self is a way to care for your relationship with yourself. Caring and being kind needs practice to become a lifelong habit. It is completely an inside job.

自分のことを大切にする習慣を持ちましょう。
体だけでなく、自分の心にも気を配りましょう。

---

many physical ways 身体的に多くの面で

99. Speak Well To Yourself

What you think about most of the time has great power in your life. You can change your thinking with how you talk to yourself in your mind; this is called self-talk. Self-talk is **the ongoing talk in your mind** you have with yourself. Self-talk runs from the first waking moment in the morning until you go to sleep at night.

Your thoughts and your self-talk are either positive or negative. You look at the world around you and what is going on and you either view it as positive or negative. Make sure your self-talk is mostly positive because your self-talk about what is going on will make you a positive or negative person.

'I have to be careful what I say to myself as my self-talk is the thing in my life that makes me happy or unhappy.'

Toni

自分自身に語りかける言葉、セルフトークは、人生において大きな力を持ちます。そのため、常にポジティブなセルフトークをすることが大切なのです。

....
the ongoing talk in your mind あなたの内なる会話

100. Success Starts With You

Success in a relationship depends on the way you think and care about yourself as well as how you think and care about the other person. A positive attitude about yourself is **one of the most important things** you can bring into your relationship. When you feel good about yourself you can then add something strong and **valuable** to a relationship.

Being happy and loving to yourself as well as the other person makes you a more balanced, happy person. When you like yourself and have a strong feeling of care and thought for yourself, you will have more care and thought for the other person **as well**.

自分を大切にするのです。
そうすれば、あなたは人にもやさしくすることができます。
自分に対してポジティブであることは、
人間関係においてとても大切なことなのです。

---

one of the most important things 一番大切なことの1つ　　**valuable** 価値のある
as well 同様に

著者紹介

Vicki Bennett ヴィッキー・ベネット
企業コンサルタント、経営コンサルタント、ライフコンサルタント。『I've Found the Keys Now Where's The Car?』『I've Read the Rules Now How Do I Play The Game?』『Life Smart and Making Dreams Come True』など、人生をより良くし、モチベーションを上げるための著書を数多く執筆。イアンと共に5人の子供を育てた。

Ian Mathieson イアン・マシスン
ビジネスコンサルタント、企業戦略家。Vickiとの共著に『The Effective Leader』(HarperCollins)、『恋と仕事にスグ効く英語』『IBCオーディオブックス:恋と仕事にスグ効く英語』(IBCパブリッシング) などがある。

ヴィッキーのポジティブリスニング
100 Keys of Love

2009年9月11日　第1刷発行

著者 ………… ヴィッキー・ベネット
　　　　　　　イアン・マシスン

発行者 ………… 浦晋亮

発行所 ………… IBCパブリッシング株式会社

〒162-0804
東京都新宿区中里町29番3号　菱秀神楽坂ビル9F
Tel. 03-3513-4511　Fax. 03-3513-4512
www.ibcpub.co.jp

印刷所 ………… 株式会社シナノ

©Vicki Bennett and Ian Mathieson 2009
©IBC Publishing, Inc. 2009
Printed in Japan

カバーデザイン　コントヨコ
カバー・本文イラスト　松尾ミユキ

落丁本・乱丁本は、小社宛にお送りください。送料小社負担にてお取り替えいたします。
本書の無断複写(コピー)は著作権法上での例外を除き禁じられています。

ISBN978-4-7946-0013-4